Fodor's InFocus

ARUBA

W9-BNA-012

12
TOP EXPERIENCES
Aruba offers terrific experiences that should be on every traveler's list. Here are Fodor's top picks for a memorable trip.

1 High-Rise Resorts
On a beautiful stretch of Palm Beach, Aruba vacationers can choose among many of the Caribbean's most lavish resorts, with deluxe spas, water-sports centers, fine restaurants, casinos, shops, and nightclubs. *(Ch. 5)*

2 Eagle Beach

Prepare to be dazzled (seriously, bring your sunglasses) by the bright white sand of Eagle Beach, which stretches far and wide on the southwestern coast. The beach is popular but rarely overcrowded. *(Ch. 3)*

3 Casinos

Aruba casinos are the real deal, with slots, table games, and sports books for plenty of action. Theaters, restaurants, bars, and cigar shops round out the entertainment. *(Ch. 7)*

4 Horseback Riding

An exciting, romantic way to explore Aruba is on horseback. Take a leisurely beach ride or survey the countryside on trails flanked by cacti, divi-divi trees, and aloe vera plants. *(Ch. 8)*

5 Barhopping Buses

Why drive to a bar when a groovy bus can pick you up at your hotel? Enjoy the journey and the destination as you're shuttled to the liveliest nightspots aboard Aruba's unique party buses. *(Ch. 6)*

6 The Bonbini Festival

Every week this festival at Fort Zoutman showcases steel pan bands and local performing artists. It's both a brisk introduction to Aruba's lively culture and a great place to meet friendly locals. *(Ch. 6)*

7 Scuba Diving

Advanced and novice divers appreciate the plentiful marine life in Aruba's clear waters. Some of the best sites are right offshore, and there are fascinating shipwrecks in both deep and shallow waters. *(Ch. 8)*

8 Sailing

Day sails to remote snorkeling spots, sunset voyages on a catamaran, and champagne-and-dinner cruises are some of the most memorable ways you can spend a day or night in Aruba. *(Ch. 8)*

9 Dining on the Beach

Open-air dining on the beach is a special island experience available at a number of Aruba restaurants. The most romantic tables are at Passions on the Beach and Flying Fishbone. *(Ch. 4)*

10 Snorkeling

Thanks to water visibility of 90 feet and closed-in sites such as Barcadera Reef, snorkelers can view many of the same underwater spectacles as divers. Huge sea fans, nurse sharks, and hawksbill turtles are common sights. *(Ch. 8)*

11 Arikok National Park

At Aruba's sprawling national park you can explore caves, play on sand dunes, or hike Mt. Yamanota, the island's highest peak. History you can see includes Arawak petroglyphs and remnants of Dutch settlements. *(Chs. 2, 8)*

12 Oranjestad

Aruba's capital is a delight to explore on foot. Pastel-painted buildings of typical Dutch design face its palm-lined central thoroughfare, and there are numerous boutiques and shops. *(Chs. 2, 9)*

CONTENTS

ABOUT THIS GUIDE

Fodor's Recommendations
Everything in this guide is worth doing—we don't cover what isn't—but exceptional sights, hotels, and restaurants are recognized with additional accolades. **Fodor's**Choice ★ indicates our top recommendations. Care to nominate a new place? Visit Fodors.com/contact-us.

.Trip Costs
We list prices wherever possible to help you budget well. Hotel and restaurant price categories from $ to $$$$ are noted alongside each recommendation. For hotels, we include the lowest cost of a standard double room in high season. For restaurants, we cite the average price of a main course at dinner or, if dinner isn't served, at lunch. For attractions, we always list adult admission fees; discounts are usually available for children, students, and senior citizens.

Hotels
Our local writers vet every hotel to recommend the best overnights in each price category, from budget to expensive. Unless otherwise specified, you can expect private bath, phone, and TV in your room. For expanded hotel reviews, visit Fodors.com.

Restaurants
Unless we state otherwise, restaurants are open for lunch and dinner daily. We mention dress code only when there's a specific requirement and reservations only when they're essential or not accepted.

Credit Cards
The hotels and restaurants in this guide typically accept credit cards. If not, we'll say so.

Top Picks
★ **Fodor's**Choice

Listings
⊠ Address
⊠ Branch address
🕮 Mailing address
☎ Telephone
🖷 Fax
⊕ Website
✉ E-mail

🎫 Admission fee
☉ Open/closed times
Ⓜ Subway
⊹ Directions or Map coordinates

Hotels & Restaurants
🏨 Hotel
🛏 Number of rooms
🍽 Meal plans

✕ Restaurant
⌂ Reservations
🏛 Dress code
🖃 No credit cards
$ Price

Other
⇨ See also
☞ Take note
🏌 Golf facilities

EXPERIENCE
ARUBA

WHAT'S WHERE

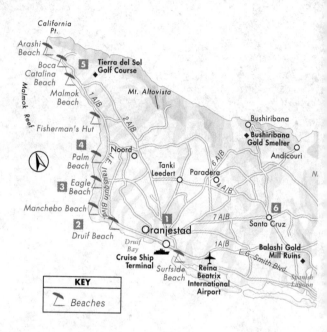

California Pt.

Arashi Beach

Boca Catalina Beach

Malmok Beach

Malmok Reef

Fisherman's Hut

5 Tierra del Sol Golf Course

Mt. Altovista

Bushiribana

◆ Bushiribana Gold Smelter

Andicouri

4 Palm Beach

Noord

Tanki Leedert

Paradera

3 Eagle Beach

Manchebo Beach

N.E. Irausquin Blvd.

1 A/B

2 A/B

6 A/B

4 A/B

2 Druif Beach

1 Oranjestad

7 A/B

6 Santa Cruz

Druif Bay

Cruise Ship Terminal

Surfside Beach

Reina Beatrix International Airport

1 A/B

L.G. Smith Blvd.

Balashi Gold Mill Ruins ◆

Spanish Lagoon

N.

KEY

⌒ Beaches

1 Oranjestad and Environs.
Aruba's capital is a great place to go for shopping, restaurants, and nightlife.

2 Druif. This area offers miles of beautiful beach that's not overdeveloped but is dominated by the sprawling Divi complex.

3 Eagle Beach. Aruba's "low-rise" hotel area is the island's best big beach.

4 Palm Beach and Noord. The island's high-rise hotels and condos are matched with an inland town.

5 Western Tip. Anchored by the California Lighthouse, this end of Aruba is quiet and remote.

6 Santa Cruz. This small town in the interior gives you a sense of how real Arubans live.

7 Arikok National Park. Nearly 20% of Aruba is covered by this sprawling park.

0   4 mi

0   6 km

C a r i b b e a n   S e a

Dos Playa

ARIKOK
NATIONAL PARK

Boca Prins
(sand dunes)

Mt. Arikok **7**

Fontein
Cave

Guadikin Cave

Miralamar

7 A/B

*Grapefield
Beach*

**Masiduri
Cave**

Baranca Sunu

*Boca
Grandi*

Mt. Yamanota

1 B

*Bachelor's
Beach*

1 A

Savaneta

San Nicolas

Seroe **10**
Colorado

*Colorado
Pt.*

1 A

8

9

Natural Bridge

*Mangel Halto
(Savaneta)*

*Santa
Largo Beach*

*Rodgers
Beach*

Baby Beach

8 Savaneta. This bustling fishing village was the first Dutch beach-head on Aruba.

9 San Nicolas. Once headquarters of the island's oil industry, this town has been reborn with public art.

10 Seroe Colorado. Almost a ghost town, this small community is on the island's eastern tip.

PLANNER

Island Activities

Since soft, sandy **beaches** and turquoise waters are the biggest draws in Aruba, they can be crowded. Eagle Beach is the best the island has to offer.

Aruba also comes alive by night, and has become a true **party hot spot**. The **casinos**—though not as elaborate as those in Las Vegas—are among the best of any Caribbean island.

Restaurants can be pricey, but many are very good.

Diving is good in Aruba, though perhaps not as great as in Bonaire.

Near-constant breezes and tranquil, protected waters have proven to be a boon for **windsurfers** and **kiteboarders,** who have discovered that conditions on the southwestern coast are ideal for their sport.

A largely undeveloped region in Arikok National Park is the destination of choice for visitors wishing to **hike** and explore some wild terrain.

Logistics

Getting to Aruba: Aruba is 2½ hours from Miami and 4½ hours from New York. Smaller airlines connect the Dutch islands in the Caribbean, often using Aruba as a hub. Travelers to the United States clear Customs and Immigration before leaving Aruba.

Nonstops: There are nonstop flights from many major American cities and seasonal from major Canadian cities. Airlines that fly nonstop from the United States to Aruba include Delta, jetBlue, American, United, Southwest, and Spirit. From Canada, Air Canada, Sunwing, and Air Transat have seasonal charters.

On the Ground

A taxi from the airport to most hotels takes about 20 minutes. It costs about $25 to hotels along Eagle Beach, $28 to the high-rise hotels on Palm Beach, and $18 to hotels downtown. They have zones, so ask first, it is a set rate—tip is not included. Public buses (⊕ *www.arubus.com*) are cheap, reliable, air-conditioned, frequent, and hit all the resorts on both main beaches, making them a great way to get around. The main terminal is right in downtown Oranjestad.

Renting a Car: Rent a car to explore independently, but for just getting to and around town, taxis are preferable, and you can use tour companies to arrange your activities. Rent a four-wheel-drive vehicle if you plan to explore the island's natural sights.

Dining and Lodging on Aruba

Aruba is known for its large, luxurious high-rise resorts and vast

1

array of time-shares. But the island also has a nice selection of smaller, low-rise resorts for travelers who don't want to feel lost in a large, impersonal hotel complex. If you're on a budget, consider booking one of the island's many apartment-style units, so you can eat in sometimes instead of having to rely on restaurants exclusively. Aruba also has Airbnb now, too.

Since the all-inclusive resort scheme hasn't taken over Aruba, as it has many other islands, you'll find a wide range of good independent and resort-based restaurant choices. There's a variety of restaurants in Oranjestad, the island's capital, but you'll also find good choices in the resort areas of Eagle and Palm beaches, as well as Savaneta and San Nicolas.

Hotel and Restaurant Costs

Prices in the restaurant reviews are the average cost of a main course at dinner or, if dinner isn't served, at lunch; taxes and service charges are generally included. Prices in the hotel reviews are the lowest cost of a standard double room in high season, excluding taxes, service charges, and meal plans (except at all-inclusives). Prices for rentals are the lowest per-night cost for a one-bedroom unit in high season.

Tips for Travelers

Currency: You probably won't need to change any money if you're coming from the United States. American currency is accepted everywhere in Aruba, though you might get some change back in local currency—the Aruban florin, also called the guilder.

Electricity: Aruba's current is 110 volts, just as in the United States.

Nightlife: Aruba is renowned for its nightlife and casinos; the legal drinking and gambling age is 18.

Traffic: Oranjestad traffic can be heavy during rush hour. Allow a bit of extra time if you're trying to get into town for dinner.

Water: You can safely drink the water in Aruba. It's one of the few places in the world to rely almost completely on desalinated seawater for drinking.

WHEN TO GO

Aruba's high season runs from early December through mid-April. During this season you're guaranteed the most entertainment at resorts and the most people with whom to enjoy it. It's also the most expensive time to visit, both for people staying a week or more and for cruise-ship passengers coming ashore. During this period hotels are solidly booked, and you must make reservations at least two or three months in advance for the very best places (and to get the best airfares). During the rest of the year hotel prices can drop 20% to 40% after April 15.

Climate

Aruba doesn't really have a rainy season and rarely sees a hurricane—one reason why the island is more popular than most during the off-season from mid-May through mid-November, when the risk of Atlantic hurricanes is at its highest. Temperatures are constant (along with the trade winds) year-round. Expect daytime temperatures in the 80s Fahrenheit and nighttime temperatures in the high 70s.

Festivals and Events

January–March: Carnival. Weeks of parties and cultural events precede this two-day street party in late February or early March.

May: Aruba Soul Beach Music Festival. This concert features interna-tional artists and takes place over two days on Memorial Day weekend at a different resort every year. ⊕ *www.soulbeach.net*

July: Aruba Hi-Winds. This wind-surfing and kiteboarding event takes place over six days, usually in late June or early July. It brings windsurfers of all skill levels from more than 30 different countries to compete off the beaches at Fisherman's Huts at Hadikurari and is considered by some to be the best in the Caribbean. ⊕ *hiwindsaruba.com*

August: Aruba Regatta. Three days of racing and parties, this is one of Aruba's annual highlights. ⊕ *aruba-regatta.com*

September: Caribbean Sea Jazz. A two-day musical extravaganza features international and local jazz and pop performers. ⊕ *caribbeanseajazz.com*

November: Aruba International Beach Tennis Tournament. The largest beach tennis competition in the Caribbean attracts competitors from all over the globe to a big party on Eagle Beach. ⊕ *arubabeachtennisopen.com*

Year-Round: Bon Bini Festival. Every Tuesday evening Fort Zoutman comes alive with music and local folk dancing.

GREAT ITINERARIES

Are you perplexed about which of Aruba's many beaches is best or how to spend your time during one of the island's rare rainy days? Below are some suggestions and a few ideas on how to create a night that completes a perfect day.

A Perfect Rainy Day

Even though Aruba is outside the hurricane belt, you may find yourself with the rare rainy day, or you might just want a break from the tropical heat if you overdid the sunbathing. That's a perfect time to explore some of the museums and the art gallery in downtown Oranjestad and ride the free eco-trolley around the newly refreshed Main Street and see what's on offer. There are lots of souvenir and high-end shopping options there, or you can head to modern, multilevel Palm Beach Plaza for all kinds of shopping, entertainment, and movies. They also have a food court and several lunch options in the immediate vicinity. You can also enjoy some first-rate pampering at one of the island's many premium spas—maybe an aloe-based treatment to soothe your overly sunned skin? This island has some of the world's best-quality aloe products. Or how about a couple's massage by the sea under a tiki hut? If you want more action, the casinos are always ready to receive you. Some are open 24

hours a day, and sometimes they offer daytime bingo as well, for something different to do.

A Perfect Day at the Beach

If you didn't bring your own, borrow or rent snorkel gear at your hotel so that you can fully appreciate the calm water and rich sea life. Arashi Beach is the island's best, but Malmok and Boca Catalina are good, too. The water here is fine for both swimming and snorkeling. If you are staying at the Renaissance hotels, snorkeling is excellent at their private lsand, but wear beach shoes (you don't need fins) as there are quite a few sea urchins. As the sun goes down, follow your ears to the music of the many happy hours at the the pool bars and beach hangouts to raise a glass to the end of the day and watch the kind of sunset over the sea this island is famous for.

A Perfect Night of Romance

Aruba is one of the most romantic places on earth, and one of its most romantic experiences is a toes-in-the-sand dinner on the beach or a sunset cruise. But there are numerous other romantic, tropical evening options. You could end with a walk—hand in hand—along the sea, or just relax on your veranda with a bottle of champagne.

ARUBA WITH KIDS

Aruba has a kid-loving culture, and its slogan "One Happy Island" extends to young visitors as well. The island is a reasonably short flight away from most of the Eastern Seaboard (about three to six hours). Though the island may not offer all of the distractions of a theme park holiday, it has more than enough to keep most kids occupied during a family vacation.

Where to Stay

Virtually all the best places for families to stay are on or along the beaches that run the length of the western side of the island. The island's east coast is rocky with rough seas and offers little in the way of accommodations. Aruba is a sun-and-sand destination, so most families will find their dollar best spent picking a hotel as close to the beach as their budget will allow. An ocean view isn't a necessity, but ease of access to one of the beaches is recommended.

Best High-Rise Resorts. Choose a high-rise resort if you want a great variety of amenities and activities. Most of Aruba's high-rise resorts offer kids' programs or dedicated kid's clubs. The **Hyatt Regency Aruba Beach Resort** offers an extensive kids' program and has many family-fun activities and the **Ritz-Carlton Aruba** has the Ritz Kidz program with seri-

ously creative activities inspired by Jean-Michel Cousteau's (Jacques Cousteau's son) and his Ocean Futures Society. **Holiday Inn Aruba** has a great dedicated kid's club and a family fun zone, too.

Best Low-Rise Resorts. Aruba's smaller low-rise properties don't offer as many amenities and water sports as the high-rises, but they provide a relaxing, laid-back vibe, and some do have kids' programs. Low-rise properties are mostly found along Eagle Beach, Manchebo Beach, and Druif Beach and are often less crowded. **Amsterdam Manor** on Eagle Beach is a good value-hotel with kitchenettes and a mini–grocery store on-site so that families can save money and enjoy a relaxing stay. At **Divi and Tamarijn Aruba All-Inclusives** on Druif Beach, children under 12 stay free when accompanied by two adults, and their kids' camp even offers Papiamento language lessons. The beach there is gorgeous, and all nonmotorized water sports are included in the price. The resorts have also erected a 30-foot tall climbing tower on the beach.

Beaches

Palm Beach is wide and offers powdery white sand, very calm waters, and plenty of nearby amenities like food and beverages. Families that want to avoid the crowds might find **Druif** and **Manchebo** beaches more to their liking, but there aren't as many options for chair rentals and refreshments. Sprawling **Eagle Beach** offers the best of all worlds with fewer crowds and a range of amenities within easy walking distance, but surf can be rough at times and current strong, so take care with little ones there.

Water Activities

Snorkeling, swimming, kayaking, and sailing are some of the things that keep families coming back to Aruba. Most hotels and condos offer inexpensive equipment rentals for a day in the water. Seasoned junior snorkelers will find the viewing pretty dull off the major beaches, so organized tours such as those offered by **De Palm Tours** and **Red Sail Sports**, and **Jolly Pirates** which explore more remote coves, may provide a better underwater experience. **De Palm Island** offers a variety of water activities for kids, including snorkeling and a water park that makes for a great day in the sun.

Though a bit pricey for larger families, the **Atlantis Submarine Tour** will likely entertain even the most jaded teen.

Splash Park right downtown is the latest fun-filled family attraction on the water.

Land Activities

The **Aruba Ostrich Farm** is an interesting short excursion that can entertain young children, but Philip's Animal Garden is where they will be entertained for hours by its many fun creatures and a huge playground. **The Butterfly Farm** is also a lovely experience for all ages, and if you go early in your holiday, you can return for free as many times as you want with your original admission voucher. The **Donkey Sanctuary Aruba** is also a must-visit. The friendly residents there love to have visitors. (Bring apples and carrots!) And for evening activities, Paseo Herencia has a gorgeous waltzing waters show three times a night in their amphitheater/courtyard and a carousel and small train. They also often have cultural shows and bouncy castles for kids, and there are movie cinemas there as well. Palm Beach Plaza Mall right behind it also has glow-in-the-dark bowling, movies, a huge video arcade, and a food court for a fun night out off the beach.

Families looking for more adventure and encounters with local wildlife can try a day of hiking at **Arikok National Park.** Eddy Croes of **Aruba Nature Sensitive Tours** is a former ranger at the park and will turn the excursion into a fun learning experience.

EXPLORING

BALMY SUNSHINE, SILKY SAND, AQUAMARINE waters, natural scenic wonders, outstanding dining, decent shopping, and an array of nightly entertainment .. Aruba's got it in spades. It's also unusual in its range of choices, from world-class oceanfront resorts equipped with gourmet restaurants and high-dollar casinos to intimate neighborhood motels and diners not far off the beach.

Aruba's wildly sculpted landscape is replete with rocky deserts, cactus clusters, secluded coves, blue vistas, and the trademark divi-divi tree. To preserve the environment while encouraging visitors to explore, the government has implemented an ongoing ecotourism plan. Initiatives include finding ways to make efficient use of the limited land resources and protecting the natural and cultural resources in such preserves as Arikok National Park and the Coastal Protection Zone (along the island's north and east coasts). An Aruba Marine Park Foundation was established to protect certain areas of the reef in 2010.

Oranjestad, Aruba's capital, is good for shopping by day and dining by night, but the "real Aruba"—with its untamed beauty—is discovered in the countryside. Rent a car, take a sightseeing tour, or hire a cab by the hour to explore. Though remote, the northern and eastern shores are striking and well worth a visit. A drive out past the California Lighthouse—which is now open to the public—or to Seroe Colorado will give you a feel for the backcountry.

The main highways are well paved, but the windward side of the island has some roads that are a mixture of compacted dirt and stones. A car is fine, but a four-wheel-drive vehicle will enable you to better navigate the unpaved interior. Remember that few beaches outside the hotel strip along Palm and Eagle beaches to the west have refreshment stands, so pack your own food and drinks. Aside from those in the infrequent restaurant, there are no public bathrooms outside of Oranjestad.

Traffic is sparse once you are away from downtown and the main tourist strips, but signs leading to sights are often small and hand-lettered (this is slowly changing as the government puts up official road signs), so watch closely. Route 1A travels southbound along the western coast, and 1B is simply northbound along the same road. If you lose your way, just follow the bend of the divi-divi trees. They always point toward the resorts.

There's rarely a day when there aren't at least three cruise ships docked in Oranjestad, so the downtown shopping area is usually bustling. Some of the smaller stores are closed on Sunday, but virtually all the larger ones are open to accommodate cruise passengers looking for bargains. Expect lines to form when ships are docked.

2

TOURS

AIR TOURS

★ Fodor's Choice **Helitours Aruba.** There's nothing like seeing
FAMILY Aruba from the air, and the cheery lemon-yellow helicopter buzzing around the island is sure to catch your eye when wandering around downtown Oranjestad. You'll find the helipad at the very end of the marina, just beyond Renaissance Marketplace. Tours are good for all ages—even babies can come aboard—and you can choose from a short Eagle Beach tour, a two-beach tour, or a longer island coastal tour. Don't forget your camera, as the views are spectacular, and the pilot is a well-informed guide, who will let you in on all the background beyond simply what you're seeing below. The helicopter can take up to three passengers and it's an exhilarating ride, well worth the expense. ⊠ *Renaissance Marketplace, Oranjestad* ✢ *At the very end of the marina at Renaissance Marketplace.* ☎ *297/594–8364* ⊕ *www.arubahelitours.net* 🖭 *From $270.*

TRAM TOURS

★ Fodor's Choice **Aruba Tram Tours.** If you'd rather ride instead of walk around the charming little capital city, then get on board one of Aruba's free eco-trolleys that loop in and arund the town all day. There are four in all, leaving the port around every half hour, and you can hop on and hop off when you please to tour the main streets, back streets, and attractions. You don't need to be a cruise passenger. All trolleys have a shaded level, and two are double-decker, offering the best views and photo ops from the top. They are a great way to acquaint yourself with the lay of the land, and they move very slowly, so you can anticipate your next stop well in advance. There are nine stops in all in a figure-eight loop. Trolleys run daily until 5 pm beginning at the cruise terminal, sometimes later if there are a lot of cruise ships in port. ⊠ *Aruba Cruise Terminal, Oranjestad* ⊕ *www.arubus.com* 🖭 *Free.*

WALKING TOURS

★ Fodor'sChoice **Aruba Walking Tours.** There is finally a wonder-
FAMILY ful walking tour of Oranjestad that highlights all the cool
attractions and historical sites of Aruba's charming, colorful
capital. Tours begin at 9 am on Monday, Wednesday, and
Friday, and cover the entire downtown at a leisurely pace in
about 2½ hours. Free Wi-Fi, bottled water, entrance to two
museums, a local food tasting, and more are all included in
the price, and the guides are well-informed, fun to be with,
and speak many languages in addition to English. Reserve
in advance if you can. ⊠ *Oranjestad* ✢ *Meet at Cosecha
Aruba* ☎ *592–5069* ⊕ *www.arubawalkingtours.com* ⌨ *$39.*

ORANJESTAD AND ENVIRONS

Aruba's capital is easily explored on foot. Its palm-lined central thoroughfare runs between old and new pastel-painted
buildings of typical Dutch design (Spanish influence is also
evident in some of the architecture). There are a lot of malls
with boutiques and shops—the Renaissance mall carries
high-end luxury items and designer fashions. A massive
renovation in downtown has given Main Street (a.k.a.
Caya G. F. Betico Croes) behind the Renaissance Marina
Resort a whole new lease on life: boutique malls, shops,
and restaurants have opened next to well-loved family-run
businesses. The pedestrian-only walkway and resting areas
have unclogged the street, and the new eco-trolley is free
and a great way to get around if you don't want to walk,
and you can hop on and hop off when you like. A new
Linear Park begins in Oranjestad and runs all the way to
the airport, providing locals and visitors alike with a scenic paved path along the sea to walk, bike, and jog and a
public square. It is Phase 1 of a long-term plan to create
the longest linear park in the Caribbean.

Aruba Aloe Museum & Factory. Aruba has the ideal conditions
to grow the aloe vera plant. It's an important export, and
there are aloe stores all over the island. The museum and
factory tour reveal the process of extracting the serum to
make many products used for beauty, health, and healing.
Guided or self-guided tours are available in English, Dutch,
Spanish, and Papiamento. There's also a store to purchase
their products on-site. Products are also available online.
⊠ *Pitastraat 115, Oranjestad* ☎ *800/952–7822* ⊕ *www.
arubaaloe.com* ⌨ *Free* ⊗ *Closed Sun.*

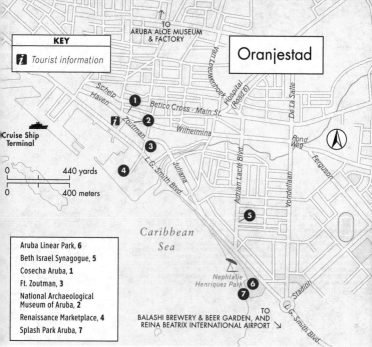

★ **Fodor's**Choice **Aruba Linear Park.** The new, recently opened
FAMILY square, Plaza Turismo, off Surfside Beach, will serve as
the anchor of the Linear Park which, when completed, will
also connect both main tourist beaches along the coast by
boardwalks and walking paths. Today, the first leg is complete—a smooth paved biking and jogging trail that runs
from downtown Oranjestad along the sea all the way to the
airport. There are many cafés, bars and snack stops along
the way, and there are also fitness pit stops with free-to-
use public fitness equipment. It has become a very popular
stretch for local fun runs and fitness intiatives, and locals
and visitors alike are loving the new easy-to-access Green
Bike rental kiosks. Much like "Bixi Bike" operations, you
can use your credit card to grab a bike and then leave it
at another stop. The new plaza is also becoming a go-to
spot for cultural events and outdoor entertainment. When
complete, the Linear Park will be the longest of its kind in
the entire Caribbean. ⊠ *Surfside Beach, Oranjestad* ⊠ *Free.*

Balashi Brewery & Beer Garden. Aruba is the only nation in
the world to make beer out of desalinated seawater, and
it's really good beer! They also make a version called Chill
with added lemon flavor and new upscale brews called Hopi

Bon ("very good" in Papiamento) and Hopi Stout ("good stout"). See how it's all done at the factory just outside Oranjestad proper and sample some of the beers afterward. There is also a lovely outdoor beer garden for lunch and drinks, sometimes offering live music during happy hour. Closed-toe shoes are required for the factory tour, which is offered Monday through Thursday. ✉ *Balashi 75, Balashi* 📞 *297/ 592–8564* 💲 *$10, includes one free beer.* ⊘ *No tours Fri., closed weekends.*

Beth Israel Synagogue. Built in 1962, this synagogue is the only Jewish house of worship on Aruba and strives to meet the needs of its Ashkenazi, Sephardic, European, North American, and South American worshippers. The island's Jewish community dates back to the opening of the oil refinery in the 1920s, when small congregations gathered in private homes in San Nicolas. The temple holds regular services on Friday at 7:30 pm, followed by kiddush; additional services are held on Saturday, Rosh Chodesh, and festivals. Visitors are always welcome, although it's best to make an appointment to see the synagogue when there's not a service. ✉ *Adrian Laclé Blvd. 2, Oranjestad* 📞 *297/582-3272* 💲 *Free except high holy days.*

★ **Fodor's**Choice **Cosecha Aruba.** One of the many historic buildings repurposed as an attraction over the past few years, this arts foundation displays only the works of local artisans. The building houses workshops, a gallery, and a design shop where visitors can purchase exquisite souvenirs. All artisans selling and showing wares here must be "Seyo" certified, a national seal that ensures that all work is locally made, of excellent quality, and reflects Aruban heritage. The beautfully restored 100-year-old mansion it's located within is worth a visit on its own. There's another Cosecha in San Nicolas. ✉ *Zoutmanstraat 1, Oranjestad* 📞 *297/578–8709* ⊕ *www.arubacosecha.com* ⊘ *Closed Sun.*

Ft. Zoutman. One of the island's oldest edifices, Aruba's historic fort was built in 1796 and played an important role in skirmishes between British and Curaçao troops in 1803. The Willem III Tower, named for the Dutch monarch of that time, was added in 1868 to serve as a lighthouse. Over time the fort has been a government office building, a police station, and a prison; now its historical museum displays Aruban artifacts in an 18th-century house. This is also the site of the weekly Tuesday night welcome party called the Bon Bini festival, with local music, food, and dance. If you visit with Aruba Walking Tours you can climb to the roof for great views. ⊠ *Zoutmanstraat, Oranjestad* ☎ *297/582–5199* ⊠ *$5* ⊘ *Closed weekends.*

★ Fodor'sChoice **National Archaeological Museum of Aruba.** Located
FAMILY in a multibuilding complex that once housed the Ecury Family Estate, this modern, air-conditioned museum showcases the island's beginnings right back to the indigenous Arawak people, including a vast collection of farm and domestic utensils dating back hundreds of years. Among the highlights are the re-created Arawak Village, multimedia and interactive presentations, and rotating exhibits of art, history, and cultural shows. ⊠ *42 Schelpstraat, Oranjestad* ✛ *Just outside Oranjestad proper* ☎ *297/582–8979* ⊕ *namaruba.org* ⊠ *Free* ⊘ *Closed Mon.*

FAMILY **Renaissance Marketplace.** The complex beside the Oranjestad marina and the park around it is the place where you're most likely to happen upon some great free entertainment, including pop-up festivals. Although there's live entertainment every night at the far end in the common area bandstand, most of the bars and cafés also invite their own bands. You'll also find a casino, movie theaters, and arty little shops that are open late. Occasionally, there's a local farmers' market or a big gala music festival going on. Even if there's no planned additional activity, it's a wonderful spot to explore in the evening to experience a truly enchanting and electrical tropical night full of colorful lights and sounds along the water. ⊠ *9 Loyd G. Smith Blvd., Oranjestad* ⊕ *www.shoprenaissancearuba.com/marketplace/* ⊠ *Free.*

FAMILY **Splash Park Aruba.** Few people realize that you can swim in downtown Oranjestad at Surfside Beach just off the new Linear Park. And now families can enjoy a unique attraction there as well. Splash Park Aruba is a huge inflatable maze of obstacles, jungle gyms, swings, slides, and climbing towers. It's a great way to cool off after downtown shopping and sightseeing with lots of aqua fun for the whole family (children six and over only.) They will also pick you up from your hotel for morning or afternoon packages and offer guided kayaking trips around the immediate area. ⊠ *Surfside Beach, Oranjestad* ☎ *297/594–1002* ⊕ *www. splashparkaruba.com* ⊠ *$15 (admission for 1 hr only); $30 (admission plus hotel pick-up).*

DRUIF

Manchebo Beach merges seamlessly with Druif Beach, resulting in a miles-long stretch of powdery sand peppered with a few low-rise resorts. This part of the island is much less crowded than Palm Beach and great for a morning or evening stroll.

EAGLE BEACH

This area is often referred to as Aruba's low-rise hotel area. It's lined with smaller boutique resorts and time-share resorts. Eagle Beach is considered one of the best beaches in the Caribbean. The white sand here seems to stretch on forever. The water is great for swimming, and there are numerous refreshment spots. Although the beach can get busy during the day, there's never a problem finding a spot, but if you're looking for shade, it's best to stick near one of the hotel bar huts along the beach.

PALM BEACH AND NOORD

The district of Noord is home to the strip of high-rise hotels and casinos that line Palm Beach. The hotels and restaurants, ranging from haute cuisine to fast food, are densely packed into a few miles running along the beachfront. When other areas of Aruba are shutting down for the night, this area is guaranteed to still be buzzing with activity. Here you can also find the beautiful **St. Ann's Church,** known for its ornate 19th-century altar. In this area Aruban-style homes are scattered amid clusters of cacti.

Bubali Bird Sanctuary. More than 80 species of migratory birds nest in this man-made wetland area inland from the island's strip of high-rise hotels. Herons, egrets, cormorants, coots, gulls, skimmers, terns, and ducks are among the winged wonders in and around the two interconnected artificial lakes that make up the sanctuary. Perch up on the wooden observation tower for great photo ops. ⊠ *J.E. Irausquin Blvd., Noord* ⊡ *Free.*

★ Fodor'sChoice **Butterfly Farm.** Hundreds of butterflies and moths
FAMILY from around the world flutter about this spectacular garden. Guided tours (included in the price of admission) provide an entertaining look into the life cycle of these insects, from egg to caterpillar to chrysalis to butterfly or moth. After your initial visit, you can return as often as you like for free

CLOSE UP

Papiamento Primer

Papiamento is a hybrid language born out of the colorful past of Aruba, Bonaire, and Curaçao. The language's use is generally thought to have started in the 17th century when Sephardic Jews migrated with their African slaves from Brazil to Curaçao. The slaves spoke a pidgin Portuguese, which may have been blended with pure Portuguese, some Dutch (the colonial power in charge of the island), and Arawakan. Proximity to the mainland meant that Spanish and English words were also incorporated.

Papiamento is roughly translated as "the way of speaking." (Sometimes the suffix -*mentu* is spelled in the Spanish and Portuguese way [-*mento*], creating the variant spelling.) It began as an oral tradition, handed down through the generations and spoken by all social classes on the islands. There's no uniform spelling or grammar from island to island, or even from one neighborhood to another. Nevertheless, it's beginning to receive some official recognition. A noteworthy measure of the increased government respect for the language is that anyone applying for citizenship must be fluent in both Papiamento and Dutch.

Arubans enjoy it when visitors use their language, so don't be shy. You can buy a Papiamento dictionary to build your vocabulary, but here are a few pleasantries to get you started:

Bon dia. Good morning.

Bon tardi. Good afternoon.

Bon nochi. Good evening/ night.

Bon bini. Welcome.

Ajo. Bye.

Te aworo. See you later.

Pasa un bon dia. Have a good day.

Danki. Thank you.

Na bo ordo. You're welcome.

Con ta bai? How are you?

Mi ta bon. I am fine.

Ban goza! Let's enjoy!

Pabien! Congratulations!

Quanto costa esaki? How much is this?

Hopi bon. Very good.

Ami. Me.

Abo. You.

Nos dos. The two of us.

Mi dushi. My sweetheart.

Ku tur mi amor. With all my love.

Un braza. A hug.

Un sunchi. A kiss.

Mi stima Aruba. I love Aruba.

2

Aruba

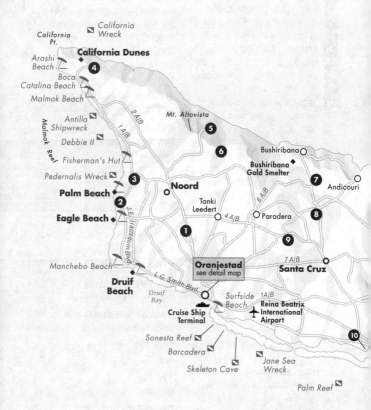

California Wreck

California Pt.

California Dunes

Arashi Beach

Boca Catalina Beach

Malmok Beach

Malmok Reef

Antilla Shipwreck

Debbie II

Fisherman's Hut

Pedernalis Wreck

Palm Beach

Eagle Beach

Manchebo Beach

Druif Beach

Druif Bay

2 A/B

1 A/B

Mt. Altovista

Noord

Tanki Leedert

4 A/B

6 A/B

Bushiribana

Bushiribana Gold Smelter

Andicouri

Paradera

Santa Cruz

7 A/B

Oranjestad
see detail map

Cruise Ship Terminal

Surfside Beach

Reina Beatrix International Airport

1 A/B

Sonesta Reef

Barcadera

Skeleton Cave

Jane Sea Wreck

Palm Reef

J.E. Irausquin Blvd.

L.G. Smith Blvd.

4

5

6

7

8

9

1

2

3

10

0   4 mi
0   6 km

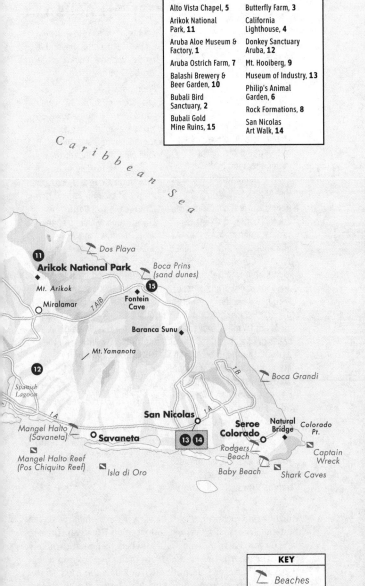

Alto Vista Chapel, **5**	Butterfly Farm, **3**
Arikok National Park, **11**	California Lighthouse, **4**
Aruba Aloe Museum & Factory, **1**	Donkey Sanctuary Aruba, **12**
Aruba Ostrich Farm, **7**	Mt. Hooiberg, **9**
Balashi Brewery & Beer Garden, **10**	Museum of Industry, **13**
Bubali Bird Sanctuary, **2**	Philip's Animal Garden, **6**
Bubali Gold Mine Ruins, **15**	Rock Formations, **8**
	San Nicolas Art Walk, **14**

Caribbean Sea

11 **Arikok National Park**

◆ Mt. Arikok

○ Miralamar

Dos Playa

Boca Prins (sand dunes)

15

Fontein Cave

7A/B

Baranca Sunu ◆

╱ Mt. Yamanota

1B

Boca Grandi

12

Spanish Lagoon

1A

San Nicolas

1A

Seroe Colorado

Natural Bridge

Colorado Pt.

Mangel Halto (Savaneta)

○ **Savaneta**

13 **14**

Rodgers Beach

Captain Wreck

Mangel Halto Reef (Pos Chiquito Reef)

Isla di Oro

Baby Beach

Shark Caves

KEY	
⛱	*Beaches*
◣	*Dive Sites*

A GOOD TOUR: WESTERN ARUBA

Western Aruba is where you'll likely spend most of your time. All the resorts and time-shares are along this coast, most of them clustered on the oceanfront strip at the luscious Palm and Eagle beaches, in the city of Oranjestad, or in the district of Noord. All the casinos, major shopping malls, and most restaurants are found in this region.

Rent a car and head out on Route 1A toward **Oranjestad** for some sightseeing and shopping. Pick up Route 1B out of town. At a large roundabout turn right and drive for about 1 km (½ mile), then make another right at the first intersection and drive for ½ km (¼ mile) until you reach the fields and factory of **Aruba Aloe**. Head back to the roundabout and pick up Route 4A. Follow this road a short way to the **Ayo and Casibari Rock Formations** where you can have lunch or dinner. Continue on 4A and follow the signs for **Hooiberg**; if you're so inclined, climb the steps of the "Haystack." Return on 4B to 6A and drive a

couple of miles to the Bushiri-bana Gold Smelter. Beyond it on the windward coast is the **Aruba Ostrich Farm**.

From here, take 6B to the intersection of Route 3B, which you'll follow into the town of **Noord**, a good place to stop for lunch. Then take Route 2B, following the signs for the branch road leading to the **Alto Vista Chapel**. Return to town and pick up 2B and then 1B to reach the **California Lighthouse**, which is open for public tours inside. In this area you can also see Arashi Beach (a popular snorkeling site and favored local haunt) and the Tierra del Sol golf course. From the lighthouse, follow 1A back toward Palm Beach. On the way, stop at the **Butterfly Farm** and the **Bubali Bird Sanctuary**.

TIMING

If you head out right after breakfast, you can just about complete the above tour in one very full day. If you want to linger in Oranjestad's shops or go snorkeling along the beach, consider breaking the tour up into two days.

during your vacation. ■ TIP→ Go early in the morning when the butterflies are most active; wear bright colors if you want them to land on you. Early morning is also when you are most likely to see the caterpillars emerge from their cocoons and transform into butterflies or moths. ⊠ *J.E. Irausquin Blvd., Palm Beach* ✚ *Across from Divi Phoenix Aruba Beach Resort* ☎ *297/586–3656* ⊕ *www.thebutterflyfarm.com* ☎ *$15.*

CLOSE UP

The Divi-Divi Tree

Like a statuesque dancer in a graceful flat-back pose, the *watapana*, or divi-divi tree, is one of Aruba's hallmarks. Oddly enough, this tropical shrub is a member of the legume family. Its astringent pods contain high levels of tannin, which is leached out for tanning leather. The pods also yield a black dye. The tree has a moderate rate of growth and a high drought tolerance. Typically it reaches no more than 25 feet in height, with a flattened crown and irregular, forked branches. Its leaves are dull green, and its inconspicuous yet fragrant flowers are pale yellow or white and grow in small clusters. Thanks to constant trade winds, the divi-divis serve as a natural compass: they're bent toward the island's leeward—or western—side, where most of the hotels are.

★ Fodor'sChoice **Philip's Animal Garden.** This nonprofit exotic
FAMILY animal rescue and rehabilitation foundation is a wonderful, child-friendly attraction you'll find just off the beaten track up in Noord. Each guest is given a bag of treats for the animal residents, which include monkeys, peacocks, an emu, an ocelot, an alpaca, and many other types of creatures you're not likely to see on Aruba. There's a large playground and ranch so little ones can run. It is also a stop on some tours. ⊠ *Alto Vista 116, Noord* ☎ *297/593–5363* ⊕ *www.philipsanimalgarden.com* ☞ *$10* ⊘ *Closed Sun.*

WESTERN TIP (CALIFORNIA DUNES)

No trip to Aruba is complete without a visit to the California Lighthouse, and it's also worth exploring the rugged area of the island's western tip. This is the transition point between Aruba's calmer and rougher coasts. Malmok Beach and Arashi Beach are popular for windsurfing and excellent for grabbing dramatic sunset photos.

Alto Vista Chapel. Meaning "high view," Alto Vista was built in 1750 as the island's first Roman Catholic Church. The simple yellow and orange structure stands out in bright contrast to its stark desertlike surroundings, and its elevated location affords a wonderful panoramic view of the northwest coast. Restored in 1953, it's still in operation today with regular services and also serves as the culmination point of the annual walk of the cross at Easter. You will see small signposts guiding the faithful to the Stations of

Alto Vista Chapel, on the windy northwest coast of Aruba, was built in 1750.

the Cross all along the winding road to its entrance. This landmark is a typical stop on most island tours. ■TIP→ Make sure to stop and buy coconut water from the famous coconut man out front. ⊠ *Alto Vista Rd., Oranjestad* ✛ *Follow the rough, winding dirt road that loops around the island's northern tip, or from the hotel strip, take Palm Beach Road through three intersections and watch for the asphalt road to the left just past the Alto Vista Rum Shop.*

★ Fodor'sChoice **California Lighthouse.** Declared a national mon-
FAMILY ument in 2015, the landmark lighthouse on the island's eastern tip has been restored to its original glory and is now open to the public. Climb the spiral stairs to discover a fabulous panoramic view and learn all about its history from the guided tour. It was named after a merchant ship that sunk nearby called the *Californian*, a tragedy that spawned its construction. Built in 1910, the lighthouse has been a famous Aruba attraction for decades, but was heretofore inaccessible. It is also a very popular spot to take wedding photos. Expensive private VIP tours are also available. ⊠ *2 Hudishibana, Westpunt* ☎ *297/586–0787* ⊕ *www.arubalighthouse.com* ⊠ *$10.*

SANTA CRUZ

Though not a tourist hot spot (by Aruba standards) this town in the center of the island offers a good taste of how the locals live. It's not architecturally interesting, but there are some intriguing little restaurants and snack shacks. Local shops offer something a bit different from the usual tourist fare, and the prices are reasonable.

Bubali Gold Mine Ruins. Out by Frenchman's Pass you can view what is left of Aruba's one-time gold rush. The historic ruins of the Bubabli gold smelter are striking against the sea and a great spot for photo ops. It's ironic that the Spanish left the island alone basically because they thought it was worthless; in fact, they dubbed it "isla inutil" (useless island) since it had no gold or silver, but locals did find some long after the Spanish left. ⊠ *Frenchman's Pass, Santa Cruz.*

Mt. Hooiberg. Named for its shape (*hooiberg* means "haystack" in Dutch), this 541-foot peak lies inland just past the airport. If you have the energy, you can climb the some 562 steps to the top for an impressive view of Oranjestad (and Venezuela on clear days). ■ TIP→ It's a very hot climb with no shade, so wear a hat, sunscreen well, and bring water. ⊠ *Santa Cruz.*

ARIKOK NATIONAL PARK AND ENVIRONS

Nearly 20% of Aruba has been designated part of Arikok National Park, which sprawls across the eastern interior and the northeast coast. The new, eco-friendly visitor center is built entirely of sustainable South American hardwood, uses solar panels for clean energy, and cools the building with an underground water basin. The park is the keystone of the government's long-term ecotourism plan to preserve Aruba's resources and showcases the island's flora and fauna. Other highlights include ancient Arawak petroglyphs, ruins of a gold-mining operation at Miralmar, and remnants of Dutch peasant settlements in Masiduri. Within the confines of the park are Mt. Arikok and the 620-foot Mt. Yamanota, Aruba's highest peak. The natural pool (conchi) is a popular snorkeling destination and a beautiful natural phenomenon.

Anyone looking for geological exotica should head for the park's caves, found on the northeastern coast. Baranca Sunu, the so-called Tunnel of Love, has a heart-shape

Aruba's divi-divi trees are always bent toward the west, toward the best beaches.

entrance and naturally sculpted rocks farther inside that look like the Madonna, Abraham Lincoln, and even a jaguar. Fontein Cave, which was used by indigenous peoples centuries ago, is marked with ancient drawings (rangers are on hand to offer explanations). Bats are known to make appearances—don't worry, they won't bother you. Although you don't need a flashlight because the paths are well lighted, it's best to wear sneakers.

★ Fodor'sChoice **Arikok National Park.** Covering almost 20% of the island's landmass, this protected preserve of arid, cacti-studded outback has interesting nature and wildlife. Start at the modern visitor center to get information on native animals and see short films about what to look out for in the park. Then take a free guided tour with a park ranger to unearth hidden secrets. Hiking maps for all levels of hikers are free, and in-depth maps of the park and its attractions are also available for download online at their website. Some trails lead to glorious seaside coastal views and you can also traverse the park by car (roads are rough, 4x4 recommended), but a guided tour will help you understand the significance of the region and help you find attractions like the caves on the northeastern coast. Baranca Sunu, the so-called Tunnel of Love, has a heart-shape entrance and naturally sculpted rocks farther inside. Fontein Cave, which was used by indigenous peoples centuries ago, is marked with ancient drawings. Bats make their home in the caves—don't worry, they

A GOOD TOUR: EASTERN ARUBA

Take Route 1A to Route 4B and visit the **Balashi gold smelter ruins**. Return to 1A and continue your drive past Mangel Halto Beach to **Savaneta**, a fishing village and one of several residential areas that have examples of typical Aruban homes. Follow 1A to **San Nicolas**, where you can meander along the main promenade and witness the incredible new art walk, pick up a few souvenirs made by local artisans and Cosecha, and grab a bite to eat at Charlie's Bar. Heading out of town, continue on 1A until you hit a fork in the road; follow the signs toward **Seroe Colorado**, with the nearby natural bridge and the Colorado Point Lighthouse. From here, follow the signs toward Rodgers Beach, just one of several area shores where you can kick back for a while. Nearby Baby Beach, with calm waters and beautiful white sand, is a favorite spot for snorkelers. You can rent some equipment from

JADS dive center there if you want to give it a whirl. To the north, on Route 7B, is Boca Grandi, a great windsurfing spot. Next is Grapefield Beach, a stretch of white sand that glistens against a backdrop of cliffs and boulder formations. Shortly beyond it, on 7B, you'll come into **Arikok National Park**, where you can explore caves and tunnels, play on sand dunes, and tackle Mt. Yamanota, Aruba's highest elevation. Farther along 7B is **Santa Cruz**, where a wooden cross stands atop a hill to mark the spot where Christianity was introduced to the islanders. Stop by the Donkey Sanctuary Aruba to say hi to these friendly critters. The same highway will bring you all the way into Oranjestad.

TIMING
You can see most of eastern Aruba's sights in a half day, though it's easy to fill a full day if you spend time relaxing on a sandy beach or exploring the trails in Arikok National Park.

won't bother you, but it's best to wear sneakers, because ground bugs can be bothersome. Park gates close at 4 pm daily, and visitors are generally not allowed in the park at all after dusk, but organized full-moon guided hikes are offered as special events. There are no facilities past the visitor center, so bring plenty of water and sunscreen and wear good shoes if you are on foot, as the terrain is very rocky. A new region near Spanish Lagoon has also been added recently as part of its protected area. ✉ *San Fuego* 70 ☎ 297/585–1234 ⊕ *www.arubanationalpark.org* 🎫 $11.

FAMILY **Aruba Ostrich Farm.** Everything you ever wanted to know about the world's largest living birds can be found at this farm and ranch. There are emus, too! A large *palapa* (palm-thatched roof) houses a gift shop and restaurant that draws large bus tours, and tours of the farm are available every half hour. Feeding the ostriches is fun, and you can also hold an egg in your hands. ⊠ *Makividiri Rd., Paradera* ☎ *297/585–9630* ⊕ *www.arubaostrichfarm.com* ⊴ *$12.*

★ Fodor'sChoice **Donkey Sanctuary Aruba.** Take a free tour of
FAMILY the island's only donkey sanctuary where volunteers help abandoned and sometimes ill wild animals enjoy a happy forever home. This is a nonprofit organization and can always use help. You can donate there or on their website, and you can even adopt a donkey—your donation goes to its annual feed and care. They are fun, friendly animals and really enjoy visitors. It's a great family outing for all ages and everyone can help with the chores if they like as well. ■ TIP→ Bring carrots and apples for a really warm welcome from the residents. ⊠ *Bringamosa, 2-Z Santa Cruz* ☎ *297/593–2933* ⊕ *main.arubandonkey.org* ⊴ *Free.*

Rock Formations. The massive boulders at Ayo and Casibari are a mystery, as they don't match the island's geological makeup. You can climb to the top for fine views of the arid countryside. The main path to Casibari has steps and handrails, and you must move through tunnels and along narrow steps and ledges to reach the top. At Ayo you can find ancient pictographs in a small cave (the entrance has iron bars to protect the drawings from vandalism). At the base of Casibari there is a café-bar-restaurant open for lunch, and their dinner at night when lit up with colored lights around the rocks is surreal. Some party bus tours stop there for dinner before continuing on their barhop journey. There is also a children's playground at Casibari. ⊕ *www.casabaricafe.com.*

SAVANETA

The Dutch settled here after retaking the island in 1816 and made this Aruba's first capital city. Today, the once sleepy little fishing village is making a quiet metamophosis into the boho chic place to stay with new overwater bungalows, ritzy little villa rentals, and even new condos on the horizon. Cosmopolitan cafés are sidling up to heritage buildings, and new eco-activities and arty pastimes are also taking hold. There is also talk of a new museum to trace the village's interesting past.

CLOSE UP

Cunucu Houses

Pastel houses surrounded by cacti fences adorn Aruba's flat, rugged *cunucu* ("country" in Papiamento). The features of these traditional houses were developed in response to the environment. Early settlers discovered that slanting roofs allowed the heat to rise and that small windows helped to keep in the cool air. Among the earliest building materials was *caliche,* a durable calcium-carbonate substance found in the island's southeastern hills. Many houses were also built using interlocking coral rocks that didn't require mortar (this technique is no longer used, thanks to cement and concrete). Contemporary design combines some of the basic principles of the earlier homes with touches of modernization: windows, though still narrow, have been elongated; roofs are constructed of bright tiles; pretty patios have been added; and doorways and balconies present an ornamental face to the world beyond.

SAN NICOLAS

During the oil refinery heyday, Aruba's oldest village was a bustling port and the island's economic hub. As demand for oil dwindled and tourism rose, attention shifted to Oranjestad and the island's best beaches. The past few years, San Nicolas has had a renaissance: every Thursday night there's Caribbean Festival, a minicarnival in the streets. There's a new ballpark, a carnival village, and a modern museum of industry in the historic old water tower. A perennial draw is the legendary Charlie's Bar & Restaurant, a family-run business that's been around since 1941. It's packed with paraphernalia left behind by generations of visitors. The main streets are now awash in outdoor murals and fabulous art thanks to the annual Aruba Art Fair, which takes place every fall, when local and international artists come to town to create permanent public works of art, which they leave behind. Take a stroll and take some fabulous photos. A branch of Oranjestad's Cosecha Art Gallery and Workshop is also located here.

★ Fodor'sChoice **Museum of Industry.** The old water tower in San Nicolas has been beautifully restored into a modern, interactive museum chronicling the different types of industries that have fueled the island's economy over the past two centuries. Phosphate, gold, oil, and aloe have all played major parts

in the island's fortunes until tourism became Aruba's main economic driver. Displays include artifacts and profiles of colorful characters who played big roles in different eras; guided tours are also offered. There is also a soundstage audiovisual room for special presentations. One of the highlights is the culture wall, a mural consisting of portraits of locals through the ages, all leading up the glassed-in walls of the old tower staircase. ⊠ *Water Tower, Bernhardstraat 164, San Nicolas* ☎ *297/584–7090* ⊕ *www.aruba.com/things-to-do/museum/industry* ⊠ *$5* ⊙ *Closed Sun.*

San Nicolas Art Walk. In the past few years San Nicolas has seen an extraordinary revitalization and beautification thanks to new art initiatives. What began as a simple mural project in 2015 has since blossomed into the establishment of an annual Aruba Art Fair to create more public art projects here. The result is incredible and gets better each year. You'll find giant iguanas made from recycled materials, glowing lionfish, and many murals. ⊠ *San Nicolas.*

SEROE COLORADO

This surreal ghost town was originally built as a community for American oil workers who came to run the Lago Refinery in the 1950s. There were 700 residents, an English-language school, a social club, a beach club, a hospital, a local newspaper, and a bowling alley. Today, organ-pipe cacti form the backdrop for the sedate white-washed cottages. Many people visit to seek out the so-called **natural bridge.** (Another more famous bridge on the other end of the island collapsed into the sea a few years ago, but there are smaller, similar formations scattered around the island, including this one.) Keep bearing east past the community, continuing uphill until you run out of road. You can then hike down to the cathedral-like formation. It's not too strenuous, but take care as you descend. Be sure to follow the white arrows painted on the rocks, as there are no other directional signs. The raw elemental power of the sea, which created this fascinating rock formation, complete with hissing blowholes, is stunning. Many tours come out there to bring visitors to snorkel at Baby Beach in front of Seroe Colorado and there is a dive operator and restaurants on the beach there as well.

3

BEACHES

THE BEACHES ON ARUBA ARE legendary: the solid seven miles of beachfront along its west coast are baby-powder-soft, blindingly white sand carpets that smile over vast expanses of clear azure water with varying degrees of surf action. The waters of Palm Beach in front of the high-rise resort strip are typically pond-still placid, whereas the waves on the low-rise resort strip on Eagle Beach are typically restless and rolling. The beaches on the northeastern side are unsafe for swimming because of strong currents and rough swells, but they are worth seeking out for their natural beauty and romantic vistas. You might see bodyboarders and kitesurfers out there, but they are typically highly skilled locals who know the conditions well. Swimming on the sunrise side of the island is best done in Savaneta at Mangel Halto and in San Nicolas at Rodger's Beach or Baby Beach, named for its toddler-friendly calm waters.

ORANJESTAD AND ENVIRONS

FAMILY **Renaissance Island.** This tiny tropical oasis is accessible only to guests of the Renaissance Marina and Renaissance Ocean Suite hotels unless you buy an expensive day-pass, which is not always available. Free boat shuttles pick up guests in the lower lobby or from the helipad in the marina. Iguana Beach is family-friendly, while Flamingo Beach is limited to adults and hosts a flock of resident flamingoes. (Children may visit the flamingoes for a photo op daily from 10 to 11 am but must have an adult present.) The waters are clear and full of colorful fish; swimming is in a protected area, and there's a full-service restaurant, a beach bar, and waiter service on the beach. Rent a cabana for more luxuries. If you book a spa treatment, you can spend the rest of the day on the island for free. **Amenities:** food and drink; toilets; showers. **Best for:** swimming; water sports; snorkeling. ⊠ *Oranjestad* ✢ *Accessible by water taxi only from the Renaissance Aruba Hotel & Marina* ⊕ *www.arubaprivateisland.com* ⊠ *Day Pass $100.*

Surfside. Accessible by public bus, car, or taxi, this little beach has come back to life just outside downtown Oranjestad with new beach bars, a paved path of the linear park passing by, and a new tourist square. It's also the spot for a new inflatable water park that also offers small sea-kayaking tours. This is an ideal spot to stop for a dip when cycling or jogging along the bike path or strolling around the town. **Amenities:** food and drink; parking (free); toilets; water sports. **Best for:** swimming; partiers; sunsets. ✉ *L.G. Smith Blvd., just before airport compound, Oranjestad.*

DRUIF

Druif Beach. Fine white sand and calm water make this beach a great choice for sunbathing and swimming. It's the base beach for the Divi collections of all-inclusive resorts, so amenities are reserved for guests. But the locals like it, too, and often camp out here as well with their own chairs and coolers. The beach is accessible by bus, rental car, or taxi, and it's within easy walking distance to many stores for food and drinks. You can also buy coupons at the front desk of both resorts if you want to purchase food and drink from their facilities. **Amenities:** food and drink; toilets; parking (free). **Best for:** swimming; water sports; partiers. ✉ *J.E. Irausquin Blvd., Druif ✤ Near the Divi resorts, south of Punta Brabo.*

★ **Fodor'sChoice Manchebo Beach** (*Punta Brabo*). Impressively wide, the white-sand shoreline in front of the Manchebo Beach Resort is the backdrop for the numerous yoga classes now taking place under the giant palapa since the resort began offering health and wellness retreats. This sand stretch is the broadest on the island; in fact you can even get a workout just getting to the water! Waves can be rough and wild there at certain times of the year, though, so mind the current and undertow when swimming. ■TIP➔ The Bucuti beach bar no longer serves walk-ins and is now reserved exclusively for guests. **Amenities:** food and drink; toilets. **Best for:** swimming; sunsets; walking. ✉ *J.E. Irausquin Blvd., Druif ✤ At Manchebo Beach Resort.*

EAGLE BEACH

★ **Fodor'sChoice Eagle Beach.** Aruba's most photographed stretch of sand, Eagle Beach is not only a favorite with visitors and locals, but also of sea turtles. More sea turtles nest here than anywhere else on the island. This pristine stretch of blinding white sand and aqua surf is ranked among the best beaches in the world. Many of the hotels have facilities on or near the beach, and refreshments are never far away, but chairs and shade palapas are reserved for resort guests only.

Amenities: food and drink; toilets; parking (free). **Best for:** sunsets; swimming; water sports. ⊠ *J.E. Irausquin Blvd., Druif ⊹ North of Manchebo Beach.*

PALM BEACH AND NOORD

Fisherman's Huts (*Hadicurari*). Beside the Ritz-Carlton, Fisherman's Huts is a windsurfer's and kiteboarder's haven. Swimmers might have a hard time avoiding all the boards going by, as this is the nexus of where the lessons take place for both sports, and it's always awash in students and experts and board hobbyists. It's a gorgeous spot to just sit and watch the sails on the sea, and lately it's become increasingly popular among paddleboarders and sea kayakers, too. Only drinks and small snacks are available at the operator's shacks. There are no restrooms, but the Ritz lobby is nearby in a pinch. **Amenities:** food and drink; parking (free). **Best for:** windsurfing; water sports. ⊠ *Palm Beach ⊹ North of Aruba Marriott Resort.*

★ **Fodor'sChoice Palm Beach.** This is the island's most populated and popular beach running along the high-rise resorts, and it's crammed with every kind of water sports activity and food and drink emporium imaginable. It's always crowded no matter the season, but it's a great place for people-watching, sunbathing, swimming, and partying; and there are always activities happening like paddleboarding, and even paddleboard yoga. The water is pond-calm, the sand powder-fine. **Amenities:** food and drink; toilets; water sports; showers. **Best for:** partiers; swimming; water sports. ⊠ *J.E. Irausquin Blvd., Palm Beach ⊹ Between Divi Phoenix Resort and Ritz-Carlton Aruba.*

WESTERN TIP

★ **Fodor'sChoice Arashi Beach.** This is the local favorite, a half-mile (1-km) stretch of gleaming white sand with a rolling surf and great snorkeling. It can get busy on weekends—especially on Sundays—with local families bringing their own picnics, but during the week it is typically quiet. Lately, however, more visitors have been discovering it since some tours and sports outfitters now stop here for kayaking and snorkeling. ■TIP→ There's a $1 fee to use the toilets here. **Amenities:** food and drink; toilets; parking (free). **Best for:** swimming; snorkeling; walking. ⊠ *Malmokweg ⊹ West of Malmok Beach, on the west end.*

Boca Catalina. A fairly isolated strip off a residential area, this tiny white-sand cove attracts snorkelers with its shallow water filled with fish and cool little caves. Swimmers will also appreciate the calm conditions. Access the water by a tiny stone staircase carved into the cliff. There aren't any facilities nearby, however, so pack provisions and your own snorkel gear. It's popular with locals on weekends. **Amenities: none. Best for:** snorkeling; swimming. ⊠ *Malmokweg* ⊹ *Between Arashi Beach and Malmok Beach, north of intersection of routes 1B and 2B.*

Malmok Beach (*Boca Catalina*). On the northwestern shore, this small, nondescript beach borders shallow waters that stretch 300 yards from shore. There are no snack or refreshment stands here, but shade is available under the thatched umbrellas. Right off the coast here is a favorite haunt for divers and snorkelers—the wreck of the German ship *Antilla,* scuttled in 1940. All the snorkel boat tours stop here for a dip as well. There is no easy access into the water from the shore; it's very rocky with sharp cliffs and steep descents. Snorkeling is best done from a boat. **Amenities: none. Best for:** solitude; snorkeling; sunsets; walking. ⊠ *J.E. Irausquin Blvd., Malmokweg.*

ARIKOK NATIONAL PARK AND ENVIRONS

Boca Prins. You'll need a four-wheel-drive vehicle to make the trek to this strip of coastline, which is famous for its backdrop of stunning sand dunes. Near the Fontein Cave and Blue Lagoon, the beach itself is small, but with two rocky cliffs and crashing waves, it's as romantic as Aruba gets. The water is rough, and swimming is prohibited. It's a perfect picnic stop. There's also a nice restaurant bar with good local specialities and, surprisingly enough, free Wi-Fi! Wear sturdy shoes, as the entrance is rocky. **Amenities:** food and drink; toilets; parking (free). **Best for:** walking; solitude. ⊹ *Off route 7A/B, near Fontein Cave.*

Dos Playa. One of the most photogenic picnic spots on the island, this beach is two coves divided by limestone cliffs. One is treasured by surfers for its rolling waves; the other looks placid but has a current that is far too strong for swimming—you have to settle for sunbathing only. The best access is by four-wheel drive, as it's within the boundaries of rugged Arikok National Park. **Amenities:** none. **Best for:** walking; solitude; surfing. ✛ *Just north of Boca Prins.*

SAVANETA

Mangel Halto (*Savaneta Beach*). With a sunken wreck near the coast and a lot to see outside the bay, this is one of the most popular spots for shore diving, but be aware that currents are strong once you're outside the cove. It's also popular for picnics, and a wooden dock and stairs into the ocean make getting into the water easy. Sea kayak tours depart from here, and some outfits offer power snorkeling and regular snorkeling as well. There are stores within easy walking distance for food and drink. There are very few palapas, but you can take shade under the many trees and mangroves. **Amenities:** none. **Best for:** snorkeling; swimming; water sports. ✉ *Savaneta* ✛ *Between Savaneta and Pos Chiquito.*

Santo Largo. Swimming conditions are good—thanks to shallow water edged by white-powder sand—but there are no facilities at this beach west of Mangel Halto. **Amenities:** none. **Best for:** swimming. ✉ *Just west of Savaneta, San Nicolas.*

SAN NICOLAS

Bachelor's Beach (*Boca Tabla*). This east-side beach is known for its white-powder sand. Snorkeling can be good, but the conditions aren't the best for swimming. **Amenities:** none. **Best for:** snorkeling; windsurfing. ✉ *East end, south of Boca Grandi.*

Boca Grandi. This is *the* choice for the island's best kiteboarders and expert windsurfers, even more so than Fisherman's Huts. But the currents are seriously strong, so it's not safe for casual swimming. It's very picturesque, though, and a perfect spot for a picnic. It's a few minutes from San Nicolas proper; look for the big red anchor or the kites in the air. But be forewarned: the condtions are not for amateurs, and there are no lifeguards or facilities nearby should you get into trouble. **Amenities:** parking (free). **Best for:** solitude; walking; windsurfing. ✉ *San Nicolas* ✛ *Near Seagrape Grove, on the east end.*

Grapefield Beach. Just North of Boca Grandi on the eastern coast, a sweep of blinding-white sand in the shadow of

Baby Beach is a great spot for the family.

cliffs and boulders is marked by an anchor-shape memorial dedicated to seamen. Pick sea grapes from January to June. Swim at your own risk; the waves here can be rough. This is not a popular tourist beach, so finding a quiet spot is almost guaranteed, but the downside of this is a complete lack of facilities or nearby refreshments. **Amenities:** none. **Best for:** solitude. ⊠ *Southwest of San Nicolas, on east end.*

SEROE COLORADO

★ Fodor'sChoice **Baby Beach.** On the island's eastern tip (near the
FAMILY refinery), this semicircular beach borders a placid bay of turquoise water that's just about as shallow as a wading pool—perfect for families with little ones. A small coral reef basin at the sea's edge offers superb snorkeling, but do not pass the barrier as the current is extremely strong outside the rocks. The JADS dive shop offers snorkel and dive rentals; there are also a full-service bar and restaurant and a new infinity pool bar. Another large bar–dining spot on the other end is called Big Mommas Grill. You can rent clamshell shade tents and lounges. **Amenities:** food and drink; showers; toilets; parking (free); **Best for:** snorkeling; swimming. ⊠ *Seroe Colorado.*

FAMILY **Rodger's Beach.** Near Baby Beach on the island's eastern tip, this beautiful curving stretch of sand is only slightly marred by its proximity to the tanks and towers of the oil refinery at the bay's far side. Swimming conditions are excellent here. It's usually very quiet during the week, so you might have the beach all to yourself, but it's a local favorite on weekends. Full facilities can be found next door at JADS dive center strip on Baby Beach. **Amenities:** food and drink; toilets; parking (free). **Best for:** swimming; solitude. ✉ *Seroe Colorado* ✛ *Next to Baby Beach*.

WHERE TO EAT

THERE ARE A FEW HUNDRED restaurants on Aruba, from elegant eateries to seafront shacks, so you're bound to find something to tantalize your taste buds. You can sample a wide range of cuisines—Italian, French, Argentine, Asian, Peruvian, and Cuban, to name a few—reflecting Aruba's extensive blend of cultures. And due to the large number of repeat tourists from the United States, American-style fare is everywhere, too. But chefs have to be creative on this tiny island because of the limited number of locally grown ingredients; beyond fresh fish and seafood, much has to be imported. But many are getting much better at providing farm-to-fork menus when possible and catering to restricted diets like gluten-free and vegan. Hot sauce made from local Madame Janette peppers is on local tables, and the seafood du jour is always a good choice just about everywhere.

Although most resorts offer better-than-average dining, don't be afraid to try one of the many excellent independent places. Ask locals about their favorite spots; some of the lesser-known restaurants offer food that's reasonably priced and definitely worth sampling. Most restaurants on the western side of the island are along Palm Beach or in downtown Oranjestad, both easily accessible by taxi or bus. If you're heading to a restaurant in Oranjestad for dinner, leave about 15 minutes earlier than you think you should; in-town traffic can get busy once beach hours are over. Some restaurants in Savaneta (Flying Fishbone) and San Nicolas (Charlie's Restaurant & Bar) are worth the trip; spring for a cab if you intend to be drinking their great cocktails and wine. Breakfast lovers are in luck. For quantity, check out the buffets at the Hyatt and Marriott. For a fabulous Sunday brunch, Windows on Aruba is the place to be.

ARUBA DINING PLANNER

DISCOUNTS AND DEALS

Aruba Gastronomic Association: Dine-Around Program and Culinary Tours (*AGA*). To give visitors an affordable way to sample the island's eclectic cuisine, the Aruba Gastronomic Association has created a Dine-Around program involving more than 30 island restaurants. Savings abound with all kinds of different packages. Other programs, such as gift certificates and coupons for dinners at the association's VIP member restaurants, are also available. You can buy Dine-Around tickets using the association's online order form, through travel agents, or at the De Palm Tours sales desk in many hotels. Participating restaurants and conditions change frequently; the AGA website has the latest information and lists all the special culinary events they offer seasonally as well. They have also added a selection of culinary tours to their offerings—minimum eight people for guided tastings at the island's top restaurants. ☎ *297/586–1266, 914/595–4788 in the U.S. ⊕ www.arubadining.com.*

Aruba Wine and Dine. Curated events and culinary experiences, including wine tastings and foodie tours, can be booked through the organization's online portal. Most events are held at a group of recommended dining spots. Each September Aruba has a weeklong Restaurant Week event with very low prices for three-course menus at all particpating dining spots. ☎ *297/586–9955 ⊕ www.arubawineanddine.com.*

PRICES AND DRESS

Aruba's elegant restaurants—where you might have to dress up a little (jackets for men, sundresses for women)—can be pricey. If you want to spend fewer florins, opt for the more casual spots, where being comfortable is the only dress requirement. A sweater draped over your shoulders will go a long way against the chill of air-conditioning. If you plan to eat in the open air, bring along insect repellent in case the mosquitoes get unruly.

RESERVATIONS

To ensure that you get to eat at the restaurants of your choice, make some calls or visit the website when you get to the island—especially during high season—to secure reservations. On Sunday you may have a hard time finding a restaurant that's open for lunch; many eateries are closed all day Monday.

TIPPING

Most restaurants add a service charge of 15%. It's not necessary to tip once a service charge has been added to the bill, but sometimes that tip is shared between all staff. If the service is good, an additional tip of 10% is always appreciated. If no service charge is included on the final bill, then leave the customary tip of 15% to 20%.

WHAT IT COSTS IN U.S. DOLLARS			
$	$$	$$$	$$$$
At Dinner	under $12	$12–$20	$21–$30	over $30

Prices are per person for a main course at dinner, excluding service charges or taxes.

TOURS

★ Fodor'sChoice **Kukoo Kunuku Wine and Tapas Tours.** Considering that the transportation for these wine-tasting and tapas-sampling tours are aboard big, brightly painted red party buses best known for their wild and crazy nightlife barhopping tours, this experience is surprisingly elegant and sophisticated. The Wine On Down The Road early-evening tour takes you to four of the island's best dining spots for a great preview of their offerings. Pickup and drop-off at your hotel is included. Locations vary, but stops are always at highly rated establishments. ☏ *297/586–2010* ⊕ *www. kukookunuku.com* ✉ *From $98.*

ORANJESTAD AND ENVIRONS

$$ ✕ **14 Bis Marketplace.** *International.* This is a good choice for breakfast, lunch, or an early dinner (they close at 6 pm) if you need to be at the Queen Beatrix airport. The owners have hit on a winning concept: food sold by the kilo from a large, market-style buffet that includes both hot and cold dishes. **Known for:** healthy options; an eclectic selection of vegan and vegetarion options; reasonable prices. ⑤ *Average main: $15* ✉ *Queen Beatrix International Airport, Reina Beatrix Airport* ☏ *297/588–1440* ⊕ *14bisaruba.com.*

★ Fodor'sChoice ✕ **Amuse Sunset Restaurant.** *International.* It's $$$$ worth the trek beyond Reina Beatrix Airport to discover why chef Patrick van der Donk and his sommelier wife, Ivette, have garnered such a loyal following of foodie fans over the years. Let them take the reins and surprise you with their choice of international fusion fare paired with fine wines in either a three- or five-course prix-fixe menu. **Known for:** stellar sunset views; surf and turf with Asian-style braised short ribs; excellent sunset views. ⑤ *Average main:* ✉ *Bucutiweg 50, Oranjestad* ☏ *297/586–5549* ⊕ *www.amusearuba.com.*

★ Fodor'sChoice ✕ **Barefoot.** *Contemporary.* Chef Gerco Aan het $$$ Rot and maitre d' and sommelier Luc Beerepoot excel at pairing creative cuisine and upscale wine choices with the

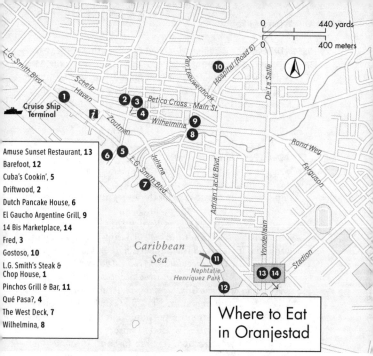

Where to Eat in Oranjestad

ultimate in a barefoot-luxury setting. Their menu of international fusion cuisine is also complemented by a choice of superb signature cocktails. **Known for:** romantic toes-in-the-sand dining; creative fusions like lobster cappucino bisque and grouper topped with mango cream cheese; sand on the floor in even the indoor dining area. ⑤ *Average main:* $26 ⊠ *L.G. Smith Blvd. 1, Oranjestad* ⊹ *Across the street from the Talk of the Town Hotel on Surfside Beach* ☎ *297/588–9824* ⊕ *www.barefootaruba.com.*

★ Fodor'sChoice ✕ **Cuba's Cookin'.** *Cuban.* This red-hot landmark
$$$ establishment in the heart of Renaissance Marketplace specializes in traditional Havana specialties and is the only spot on Aruba where you can enjoy Cuban breakfast and an authentic Cuban sandwich for lunch. Their boast of having the best mojitos in town is a fair claim, and there's even a suprisingly good selection of gluten-free, vegetarian, and vegan fare on offer as well. **Known for:** melt-in-your-mouth ropa vieja (Cuba's national skirt steak dish); hot live music and alfresco dancing; an impressive selection of orginal Cuban art. ⑤ *Average main:* $28 ⊠ *Renaissance Marketplace, L.G. Smith Blvd. 82, Oranjestad* ☎ *297/588–0627* ⊕ *www.cubascookin.com.*

$$$ ✕ **Driftwood.** *Caribbean.* Opened in 1986, this rustic, nauti-
FAMILY cal-themed restaurant is owned and operated by the Mer-
ryweather family. It's justifiably famous for serving up the
freshest catch-of-the-day caught by the owners themselves.
Known for: family-recipe, hearty fish soup; boat-to-table
fresh fish and other seafood; friendly service and warm atmo-
sphere. ⑤ *Average main: $30* ✉ *Klipstraat 12, Oranjestad*
☎ *297/583–2515* ⊕ *www.driftwoodaruba.com* ⊘ *Closed Sun.*

$$ ✕ **Dutch Pancake House.** *Dutch.* Though widely considered the
FAMILY best breakfast spot in Aruba, this restaurant offers much
more. Dutch pancakes are unlike North American-style
flapjacks since they can be both savory and sweet, offering
opportunities for breakfast, lunch, and dinner. **Known for:**
over 50 styles of sweet and savory Dutch-style pancakes;
a surprising selection of excellent schnitzels; consistently
good-quality fare and friendly service. ⑤ *Average main: $15*
✉ *Renaissance Marketplace, L.G. Smith Blvd. 9, Oranjestad* ☎ *297/583–7180* ⊕ *www.thedutchpancakehouse.com.*

$$$$ ✕ **El Gaucho Argentine Grill.** *Steakhouse.* Aruba's original go-to
FAMILY Mecca for carnivores since 1977, El Gaucho is famous for
meat served in mammoth portions. Though to be honest,
it's not all about meat; seafood platters are something to
consider as well. **Known for:** the famous 16-ounce Gaucho steak; the largest shish kebab on the island; strolling
musicians who create a fun and boisterous atmosphere.
⑤ *Average main: $40* ✉ *Wilhelminastraat 80, Oranjestad*
☎ *297/582-3677* ⊕ *www.elgaucho-aruba.com* ⊘ *Closed Sun.*

$$$$ ✕ **Fred.** *International.* One of the former "fools" of 2 Fools
and a Bull, chef Fred Wanders decided to open his own, similar chef's table experience in downtown Oranjestad. Bring
your sense of culinary adventure, and let Fred and his front-
man Tim delight you with a five-course surprise menu of
their choosing in an intimate (max. 16 people) setting that
is more akin to having dinner at a friend's home. **Known
for:** an intimate and excellent dining experience; creative
international cuisine; reservations required, and adults-
only. ⑤ *Average main:* ✉ *Wilhelminastraat 18, Oranjestad*
⊹ *Upstairs from Que Pasa restaurant* ☎ *297/565–2324*
⊕ *www/fredaruba.com* ⊘ *Closed Sat. and Sun.*

$$$ ✕ **Gostoso.** *Caribbean.* Locals adore the magical mixture of
FAMILY Portuguese, Aruban, and international dishes on offer at
this consistently excellent establishment. The decor walks
a fine line between kitschy and cozy, but the atmosphere
is relaxed and informal and outdoor seating is available.
Known for: hearty Venezuelan-style mixed grill; large
choice of authentic Aruba stobas (stews); popular local

Yo, Ho, Ho, and a Cake of Rum

When Venancio Felipe Bareno came to Aruba from Spain more than half a century ago, he probably didn't think his family's rum-cake recipe would make culinary history. Now the sweet little dessert is known around the world. Bright Bakery owner Franklin Bareno, his nephew, packages the pastry for local and international sales. The history of this island favorite is printed on the side of the box. Made with Aruban Palmeira rum, Natural Bridge Aruba's rum cake makes the perfect gift for folks back home. Available in two sizes, the vacuum-sealed cakes stay fresh for up to six months. The company is registered in the United States, so you can transport the cakes through customs.

hangout. $ *Average main: $28* ⊠ *Caya Ing Roland H. Lacle 12, Oranjestad* ☎ *297/588–0053* ⊕ *www.gostosoaruba. com* ⊘ *Closed Mon.*

$$$$ ✕ **L.G. Smith's Steak & Chop House.** *Steakhouse.* A study in teak, cream, and black, this fine steak house offers some of the best beef on the island. Subdued lighting and cascading water create an elegant atmosphere, and the view over the harbor makes for an exceptional dining experience. **Known for:** USDA-certified Angus beef; excellent wine list and stellar signature cocktails; sophisticated Sunday brunch. $ *Average main: $37* ⊠ *Renaissance Aruba Marina Resort & Casino, L.G. Smith Blvd. 82, Oranjestad* ☎ *297/523–6195* ⊕ *www.lgsmiths.com.*

★ **Fodor's**Choice ✕ **Pinchos Grill & Bar.** *Eclectic.* One of the most
$$$ romantic settings on the island is highlighted by enchanting twinkling lights strung over the water on a pier. *Pinchos* ("skewers" in Spanish) offers a fairly extensive menu of both meat and seafood skewers in addition to more creative main courses. Boursin-and-apple-stuffed pork tenderloin and fishcakes with pineapple-mayonnaise dressing and tomato salsa also keep customers coming back for more. **Known for:** romantic pier-side atmosphere; signature sangria; excellent personalized service. $ *Average main: $26* ⊠ *L.G. Smith Blvd. 7, Oranjestad* ☎ *297/583–2666* ⊘ *No lunch.*

$$$ ✕ **Qué Pasa?** *Eclectic.* This funky eatery is also part art gallery, a place where diners can view and hopefully appreciate the colorful, eclectic works of local artists while enjoying a meal or savoring a drink. Despite the name, the menu here is not Mexican but much more international, including good

Most Aruba restaurants are casual and fun places for a drink and a meal.

sashimi, rack of lamb, and fish dishes (the latter especially good). **Known for:** colorful decor and original Aruban artwork; an eclectic assortment of international dishes; fun and friendly atmosphere. ⑤ *Average main: $22* ⊠ *Wilhelminastraat 18, Oranjestad* ☎ *297/583–4888* ⊕ *www.quepasaaruba.com* ⊙ No lunch.

$$ **FAMILY** ✕ **The West Deck.** *Caribbean.* Opened by the same people who own Pinchos, this fun, friendly, wood-decked grill joint offers casual fare like barbecue ribs and grilled shrimp by the dozen, as well as Caribbean bites like jerk wings, fried *funchi* (like a thick polenta) with Dutch cheese, and West Indian samosas. There are some surprisingly snazzy dishes too like lobster/crab cocktail with red grapefruit and cognac cream drizzle. **Known for:** a great pit-stop along the Linear Park; Beer-Ritas (a full bottle of beer served upside down in a big margarita); superb sunset views on Surfside Beach. ⑤ *Average main: $15* ⊠ *L. G. Smith Blvd., at Governor's Bay, Oranjestad* ☎ *297/587-2667* ⊕ *www.thewestdeck.com.*

★ **Fodor's**Choice ✕ **Wilhelmina.** *International.* Chef Dennis Daat-**$$$$** selaar has been a well-known culinary mover and shaker on Aruba for years, so when he set out to create a chic urban Oranjestad enclave to showcase his talents, everyone knew it would be all about the food—and it is. Choose from a simple and elegant indoor dining area or a tropical outdoor garden oasis to sample from the creative international menu. **Known for:** creative takes on conventional dishes like a signature salad with rock lobster and scallops; excel-

Aruba's Spicy Cuisine

Arubans like their food spicy, and that's where the island's famous Madame Janette sauce comes in handy. It's made with Scotch bonnet peppers (similar to habanero peppers), which are so hot, they can burn your skin when they're broken open. Whether they're turned into *pika*, a relishlike mixture made with papaya, or sliced thin into vinegar and onions, these peppers are sure to set your mouth ablaze. Throw even a modest amount of Madame Janette sauce into a huge pot of soup, and your taste buds will tingle. (Referring to the sauce's spicy nature, Aruban men often refer to an attractive woman as a "Madame Janette.")

To tame the flames, don't go for a glass of water, as capsaicin, the compound in peppers that produces the heat, isn't water soluble. Dairy products (especially), sweet fruits, and starchy foods such as rice and bread are the best remedies.

4

lent selection of fine wines; exotic mains like Surinamese sea bass and Indonesian-style roast pork. ⑤ *Average main: $36* ⊠ *Wilhelmenastraat 74, Oranjestad* ☎ *297/583–7445* ⊕ *www.wilhelminaruba.com* ⊗ *Closed Mon.*

DRUIF

★ Fodor'sChoice × **The Chophouse.** *International.* Low-key ele-
$$$$ gance and soft piano music set the stage for this indoor enclave, where meaty chops are king and classic silver service (including dishes flambéed tableside) is still in vogue. Beyond the vast selection of grilled meats, the menu also includes such local specialties as Aruban *stoba* (stew) and keshi yena, as well as a few gluten-free vegetarian, vegan, and seafood dishes. **Known for:** premium steaks and chops; predominately organic and sustainable fare; elegant old-world atmosphere. ⑤ *Average main: $35* ⊠ *Manchebo Resort, J.E. Irausquin Boulevard 55, Druif* ☎ *297/582–3444* ⊕ *www.thechophousearuba.com.*

★ Fodor'sChoice × **Elements.** *Contemporary.* A stellar spot with
$$$$ stunning seaside views, Elements embodies the resort's reputation for promoting green living and a healthy lifestyle. The wide-ranging menu of internationally flavored dishes includes many organic, vegan, vegetarian, and gluten-free choices, and ingredients are locally sourced whenever possible. **Known for:** special Monday Aruban nights with a prix-fixe local specialty menu; romantic surfside atmo-

sphere; credit cards only (no cash). ⓢ *Average main: $40* ✉ *Bucuti and Tara Beach Resort, L. G. Smith Blvd. 55B, Eagle Beach* ☎ *297/583–1100* ⊕ *www.elementsaruba.com.*

$$$ ✕ **Twist of Flavors.** *International.* A glassed-in oasis in the
FAMILY   Alhambra Mall offers big and tasty surprises on an eclectic menu that ranges from Dutch pancakes to burgers to Asian specialties to Caribbean-inspired seafood. Even better: everything is done exceedingly well. **Known for:** Sunday Caribbean seafood nights with a steel band; kaleidescope of flavors from around the world; fun and friendly atmosphere. ⓢ *Average main: $22* ✉ *Alhambra Mall, J.E. Irausquin Blvd 47, Druif* ☎ *297/280–2518* ⊕ *www.twistofflavorsaruba.weebly.com.*

★   Fodor'sChoice ✕ **Windows on Aruba.** *International.* This stylish,
$$$$ modern restaurant overlooking Divi Golf Village offers a contemporary American-influenced menu of primarily steak and seafood. Floor-to-ceiling windows surround the restaurant on all sides and look out onto both the sea and sunset as well as a two-story atrium. **Known for:** elegant prix-fixe Sunday brunch; seasonal menu specialties; panoramic sunset views. ⓢ *Average main: $40* ✉ *Divi Village Golf Resort, J.E. Irausquin Blvd. 41, Druif* ☎ *297/523–5017* ⊕ *www.windowsonaruba.com.*

EAGLE BEACH

$$ ✕ **Asi es mi Peru.** *Peruvian.* Owner Roxanna Salinas has created an authentic Peruvian-style dining spot to share a taste of her home with locals and visitors alike. Authentic specialities are artfully served in a warm and colorful enclave, and a portion of proceeds from the wares sold at the on-site Peruvian craft market go to a local Aruban cancer foundation as well. **Known for:** Peruvian-style ceviche made tableside; lomato saltado (salted beef strips served stir-fry style); great Pisco sours. ⓢ *Average main:* ✉ *Paradise Beach Villas, J.E. Irausquin Boulevard 64, Eagle Beach* ☎ *592–5669* ⊕ *www.asiesmiperuenaruba.com* ⊘ *No dinner Mon.*

★   Fodor'sChoice ✕ **The Kitchen Table by White.** *Contemporary.*
$$$$ At perhaps one of the most exciting dining concepts on the island, award-winning chef Urvin Croes, famous for his avant-garde modern cuisine, presides over a one-table restaurant that seats only 16 people for multicourse dinners (with optional wine pairings). The evening kicks off with a sunset cocktail on the patio and then moves to the open kitchen, where chef Croes provides an excellent explana-

tion of each course as he creates it. **Known for:** creative seasonal cuisine; mostly locally sourced ingredients; reservations absolutely required well in advance. ⑤ *Average main: $100* ⊠ *The Blue Residences, J. E. Irausquin Blvd. 266, Eagle Beach* ☎ *297/593–2173* ⊕ *www.thekitchentablebywhite.com.*

$$$ ✕ **Mango's.** *International.* The main dining spot at Amsterdam Manor is a casual, alfresco affair that showcases international dishes and entertainment on a variety of theme nights. On those nights, specific cuisines, such as Italian or French are highlighted, but it's the new Tuesday "Local Fishermen" night that's really pulling in the crowds. **Known for:** specialty-themed buffets; congenial staff and festive atmosphere; interesting selection of "reef and ranch" combos for the less inquisitive. ⑤ *Average main: $25* ⊠ *Amsterdam Manor Beach Resort, J. E. Irausquin Blvd. 252, Eagle Beach* ☎ *297/527–1100* ⊕ *www.mangos-restaurant-aruba.com.*

$$$$ ✕ **Passions on the Beach.** *Caribbean.* Every night the weather allows, Amsterdam Manor Beach Resort transforms the area of Eagle Beach in front of the hotel into a magical, romantic, torchlit dining room. Imaginative creations are as beautiful as they are delicious, mostly "reef cuisine," as the main courses lean toward seafood, though meat lovers also are well-indulged. **Known for:** signature seafood dishes like the "seven seas parade" of lobster, mahi-mahi, shrimp, and grouper; creative cocktails; consistently excellent service. ⑤ *Average main: $32* ⊠ *Amsterdam Manor Beach Resort, J.E. Irausquin Blvd. 252, Eagle Beach* ☎ *297/527–1100* ⊕ *www.passions-restaurant-aruba.com.*

★ Fodor'sChoice ✕ **Screaming Eagle.** *International.* Though diners **$$$$** may be initially lured to this elegant international eatery for the novel opportunity to dine in an actual bed, it's the exquisite culinary experiences created by award-winning chef Erwin that has them constantly returning for more. The talent of their barkeeps has also garnered a loyal clientele, who are drawn to the classy lounge for creative cocktails. **Known for:** über-romantic dining in canopied lounge beds; a rotating menu of exciting seasonal specialties from northern Europe; Australian Wagyu beef with Parmesan truffle gnocchi and foamy garlic sauce. ⑤ *Average main: $45* ⊠ *J. E. Irausquin Blvd. 228, Eagle Beach* ☎ *297/587–8021* ⊕ *www.screaming-eagle.net.*

$$ ✕ **Tulip Caribbean Brasserie.** *International.* This casual, partially alfresco almost-beach restaurant is across the street from the ocean, offering a global menu of dishes, including

Indonesian, Jamaican, and French favorites. Service is fast and friendly, and the fare is reasonably priced and satisfying. **Known for:** authentic keshi yena, Aruba's national stuffed cheese dish; Dutch speciality snacks; large portions for good prices. ⑤ *Average main: $20* ⊠ *MV Eagle Beach, J. E. Irausquin Blvd. 240, Eagle Beach* ☎ *297/587–0110* ⊕ *www.tulip-restaurant-aruba.com.*

PALM BEACH AND NOORD

$$$$　✕**2 Fools and a Bull.** *International.* Friends Pauly and Bas have teamed up to offer an intimate evening of culinary entertainment that plays like a fun dinner party with friends rather than something you pay for. At most, 16 guests are assembled around the U-shaped communal dinner table for a five-course culinary adventure. **Known for:** an intimate chef's table experience; perfect wine pairings; adults-only with reservations required far in advance. ⑤ *Average main: $110* ⊠ *Palm Beach 17, Noord* ☎ *297/586–7177* ⊕ *www. 2foolsandabull.com* ⊘ *Closed weekends.*

$$$$　✕**Aqua Grill.** *Seafood.* Aficionados flock here to enjoy a wide selection of seafood and fish in a New England–style decor. Dishes like smoked swordfish and grilled red snapper served with a mango salsa are top of the list, and they also nod to a New England feel with Maine lobster. **Known for:** daily fresh seafood, either from local fishermen or flown in; massive raw bar; consistently high-quality specials. ⑤ *Average main: $32* ⊠ *J.E. Irausquin Blvd. 374, Palm Beach* ☎ *297/586–5900* ⊕ *www.aqua-grill.com.*

★　Fodor'sChoice ✕**Atardi.** *International.* This rollicking beach bar
$$$$　by day morphs into a surprisingly romantic pop-up, toes-in-the-sand dining spot as soon as the sun begins to set. Fresh fish and seafood and superb service make this place worth the wait for reservations; they are strongly recommended since there are not many tables. **Known for:** torchlit, seaside dining; excellent and attentive personal service; excellent fish and seafood, and memorable bouillabaisse. ⑤ *Average main: $40* ⊠ *Aruba Marriott Resort, L. G. Smith Blvd. 101, Palm Beach* ☎ *297/520–6537* ⊕ *www.marriott.com.*

$$　✕**Bavaria Food & Beer.** *German.* A variety of German beers, schnitzel, and bratwurst presented in a true beer-hall setting are guaranteed to provide that Oktoberfest feeling. The hearty cuisine is paired with over 20 different types of beer by owners who take their imbibing seriously. **Known for:** German cuisine served in an "oom-pa-pa" atmosphere; fun and friendly crowd of locals and visitors; outdoor

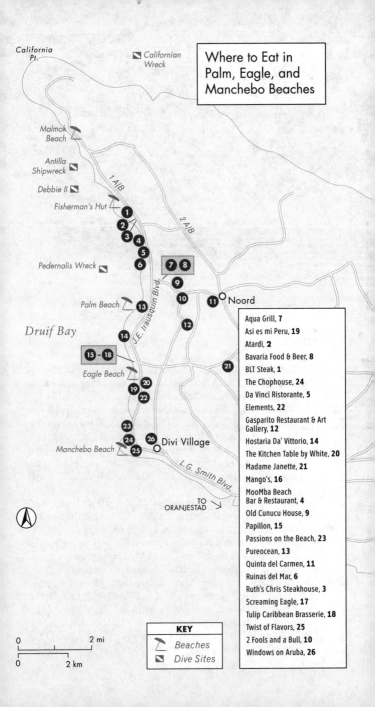

Where to Eat in Palm, Eagle, and Manchebo Beaches

California Pt.

Californian Wreck

Malmok Beach

Antilla Shipwreck

Debbie II

Fisherman's Hut

1 A1B

2 A1B

Pedernalis Wreck

Palm Beach

Druif Bay

J.E. Irausquin Blvd.

Noord

Eagle Beach

Manchebo Beach

Divi Village

L.G. Smith Blvd.

TO ORANJESTAD

KEY

⛱ Beaches

◣ Dive Sites

0 — 2 mi

0 — 2 km

Aqua Grill, **7**

Asi es mi Peru, **19**

Atardi, **2**

Bavaria Food & Beer, **8**

BLT Steak, **1**

The Chophouse, **24**

Da Vinci Ristorante, **5**

Elements, **22**

Gasparito Restaurant & Art Gallery, **12**

Hostaria Da' Vittorio, **14**

The Kitchen Table by White, **20**

Madame Janette, **21**

Mango's, **16**

MooMba Beach Bar & Restaurant, **4**

Old Cunucu House, **9**

Papillon, **15**

Passions on the Beach, **23**

Pureocean, **13**

Quinta del Carmen, **11**

Ruinas del Mar, **6**

Ruth's Chris Steakhouse, **3**

Screaming Eagle, **17**

Tulip Caribbean Brasserie, **18**

Twist of Flavors, **25**

2 Fools and a Bull, **10**

Windows on Aruba, **26**

Jumbo shrimp are a delicious staple at Madame Janette's.

beer garden suitable for large groups. $ *Average main: $20* ⊠ *Palm Beach 186, Noord* ☎ *297/736–4007* ⊕ *www. bavaria-aruba.com* ⊗ *Closed Sun.*

$$$$ ✕ **BLT Steak.** *American.* Though this fairly new restaurant in the Ritz-Carlton is designed to replicate a New York–style steak house, the stellar sunset views are unmistakably Caribbean. Chef Luis is a master at meat, and his daily blackboard specials can't help but be inspired by the bounty of the sea, so pescatarians will always be just as happy as carnivores. **Known for:** 28-day, dry-aged porterhouse for two; excellent American wagyu beef; signature warm popovers served with an eclectic choice of dipping sauces. $ *Average main: $50* ⊠ *Ritz-Carlton Aruba, L.G. Smith Blvd 107, Palm Beach* ☎ *297/527–2222* ⊕ *www. ritzcarlton.com.*

★ Fodor'sChoice ✕ **Da Vinci Ristorante.** *Italian.* Don't let the rustic decor fool you: this is not your average Italian resort eatery, though it's an inviting choice for large groups. Da Vinci pulls out all the stops to present a seriously upscale, authentic, and creative menu of Mediterranean favorites. **Known for:** creative Italian fare such as crab-and-lobster cannelloni; excellent wine cellar; family-friendly atmosphere. $ *Average main: $35* ⊠ *Holiday Inn Resort Aruba, J.E. Irausquin Blvd. 230, Palm Beach* ☎ *297/586–3600* ⊕ *www.ihg.com.*

$$$$
FAMILY

$$$ ✕ **Gasparito Restaurant & Art Gallery.** *Caribbean.* This enchanting hideaway can be found in a beautifully

The Goods on Gouda

Each year Holland exports more than 250,000 tons of cheese to more than 100 countries, and Gouda (the Dutch pronounce it *how*-da) is one of the most popular. Gouda, named for the city where it's produced, travels well and gets harder, saltier, and more flavorful as it ages. There are six types of Gouda: young (at least 4 weeks old), semi-major (8 weeks old), major (4 months old), ultra-major (7 months old), old (10 months old), and vintage (more than a year old). When buying cheese in shops in Aruba, look for the control seal that confirms the name of the cheese, its country of origin, its fat content, and that it was officially inspected.

restored 200-year-old *cunucu* (country) house, where you can dine indoors or out. Aruban specialties including keshi yena and Gasparito chicken (with brandy, white wine, pineapple, and four secret ingredients) are on the menu, the latter with a sauce passed down through the owner's family. **Known for:** a unique country house setting that is part art gallery; time-honored Aruban specialties; very limited seatings with required reservations. Ⓢ *Average main: $25* ⊠ *Gasparito 3, Noord* ☎ *297/594–2550* ⊕ *www.gasparito.com* ⊗ *Closed Sun.*

$$$ ✕ **Hostaria Da' Vittorio.** *Italian.* At one of Aruba's most celebrated Italian eateries, part of the fun at this family-oriented spot is watching chef Vittorio Muscariello prepare authentic Italian regional specialties in his open kitchen. The staff helps you choose wines from the extensive list and recommends portions of hot and cold antipasti, risottos, and pastas. Ⓢ *Average main: $28* ⊠ *L. G. Smith Blvd. 380, Palm Beach* ☎ *297/586–3838* ⊕ *www.hostariavittorio.com.*

$$$$ ✕ **Madame Janette.** *European.* The food at this rustic restaurant, named after the Scotch bonnet pepper called Madame Janette in Aruba, is surprisingly not Caribbean spicy, but French-inspired from the classically trained chef. Though many dishes are infused with Caribbean flavors, especially fish and seafood, you'll find a lot of classic sauces served with the meats. **Known for:** top-quality meat and seafood; craft beers and even a beer sommelier; specials that focus on local seasonal ingredients. Ⓢ *Average main: $35* ⊠ *Cunucu Abao 37, Cunucu Abao* ☎ *297/587–0184* ⊕ *www.madame-janette.info* ⊗ *Closed Sun. No lunch.*

$$$ ╳**MooMba Beach Bar & Restaurant.** *International.* Best known as a beach party spot, this popular restaurant also has very good food. Dinner under the giant palapa is first-rate, as is lunch—particularly since it's the perfect place for people-watching along Aruba's busiest beach. **Known for:** massive all-you-can-eat barbecue buffet on Friday and Sunday; catch-of-the-day topped in signature sauce; one-pound racks of honey-glazed ribs. ⑤ *Average main: $25* ✉ *J. E. Irausquin Blvd. 230, Palm Beach* ☎ *297/586–5365* ⊕ *www.moombabeach.com.*

$$$ ╳**Old Cunucu House.** *Caribbean.* Since the mid-1990s executive chef Ligia Maria has delighted diners with delicious and authentic *crioyo* (local) cuisine in a rustic and cozy traditional cunucu house. Try the house version of Aruba's famous keshi yena—chicken, raisins, olives, cashews, peppers, and rice in a hollowed-out Gouda rind—or thick, hearty *stobas* (stews) of goat or beef. **Known for:** secret family recipes of traditional Aruba cuisine; hearty portions and good prices; family-run and family-friendly atmosphere. ⑤ *Average main: $21* ✉ *Palm Beach 150, Palm Beach* ☎ *297/586–1666* ⊕ *www.theoldcunucuhouse.com* ⊙ *Closed Sun.*

$$$$ ╳**Papillon.** *French.* The jailhouse theme may take you aback (it's inspired by the famous Devil's Island prisoner Henri Charrière), but the popular landmark spot on the strip will win you over with its delicious French-Caribbean fusion cuisine. The menu includes both classics like frogs' legs, escargots, and French onion soup as well as duck with passionfruit sauce and local snapper with grilled shrimp and a creole sauce. **Known for:** classic French old-school cuisine with a slight Caribbean twist; bargain-priced, early-bird prix-fixe menu; rotating monthy themed specials. ⑤ *Average main: $35* ✉ *J. E. Irausquin Blvd. 348A, Palm Beach* ☎ *297/586–5400* ⊕ *www.papillonaruba.com.*

$$$ ╳**Pureocean.** *Contemporary.* Divi Phoenix's signature dining spot offers a menu of continental favorites with a Caribbean twist. You can enjoy fish, steak, and seafood beachside in the bistro or with toes in the sand mere steps from the sea. **Known for:** romantic seaside dinners; a wide selection of international fare; shareable apps and small plates like quinoa shrimp fritters. ⑤ *Average main: $25* ✉ *Divi Aruba Phoenix Beach Resort, J. E. Irausquin Blvd. 75, Palm Beach* ☎ *297/586–6066* ⊕ *www.diviresorts.com/pure-restaurants.htm.*

★ Fodor'sChoice ╳**Quinta del Carmen.** *Dutch.* Quinta del Carmen
$$$$ is set in a beautifully restored 100-year-old mansion with stunning manicured lawns and a lovely outdoor courtyard.

The cuisine here is best defined as modern Caribbean-Dutch with a few traditional Dutch favorites, like cheese croquettes and mushrooms and cream, appearing on the menu as "Grandma's favorites." The watermelon salad is sweet, salty, and perfectly refreshing, and the *sucade-lappen* (flank steak stewed in red wine and herbs) has a depth of flavor that comes from hours in the pot. **Known for:** upscale Dutch comfort food; creative seafood like shrimp piña colada; gorgeous antique mansion setting full of avant-garde art. ⑤ *Average main: $35* ⊠ *Bubali 119 Aruba, Noord* ☎ *297/587–7200* ⊕ *www.quintadelcarmen.com* ⊘ *No lunch.*

$$$$ ✕ **Ruinas del Mar.** *Caribbean.* This scenic spot is famous for its gorgeous circuit of waterfalls cascading around stone "ruins" that offers the ideal romantic setting for a quiet dinner for two. Specialties include stone-hearth-cooked items from around the world. **Known for:** lavish Sunday champagne brunch; theme nights including Land & Sea Mondays, Lobster Wednesdays, and Wine Saturdays; the resident black swans. ⑤ *Average main: $39* ⊠ *Hyatt Regency Aruba Beach Resort and Casino, J.E. Irausquin Blvd. 85, Palm Beach* ☎ *297/586–1234* ⊕ *www.aruba. hyatt.com* ⊘ *No lunch. No dinner Sun.*

$$$$ ✕ **Ruth's Chris Steakhouse.** *American.* This American steak house chain has been a popular fixture of the Aruba Marriott for years and continues to draw locals and visitors in droves. It is a no-nonsense carnivore's delight with the focus on top-quality steak, steak served with sizzling melted butter. **Known for:** top-quaility of prime beef; the famous dipping trio for steaks: black truffle buttter, shiitake demi-glace, and honey soy glaze; chopped salad with bacon, eggs, lemon basil dressing, and crispy onions. ⑤ *Average main: $45* ⊠ *Aruba Marriott Resort and Stellaris Casino, L.G. Smith Blvd. 103, Palm Beach* ☎ *297/520–6600* ⊕ *www.ruthchris.com.*

WESTERN TIP (CALIFORNIA DUNES)

$$$$ ✕ **Faro Blanco.** *Italian.* Next to the iconic California lighthouse in the former lighthouse-keeper's home, this restaurant is best known for its upscale Italian fare and grand open-air terrace overlooking the rugged west coast seascape. The restaurant is open all day, but it's renowned for sunset views, when reservations are a must. **Known for:** stunning sunset views; classics like osso bucco and calamari; filetto alla trattoria steak topped with red wine, brown sugar, cloves, cinnamon, sliced oranges, and fresh

Where to Eat Elsewhere on Aruba

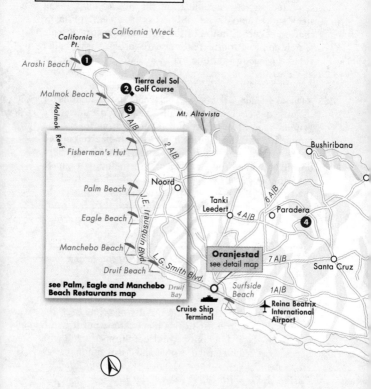

Casibari Cafe, **4**

Charlie's Restaurant
& Bar, **8**

Faro Blanco, **1**

Flying Fishbone, **6**

O'Neil Caribbean
Kitchen, **7**

The Restaurant at
Tierra del Sol, **2**

White Modern
Cuisine, **3**

Zeerovers, **5**

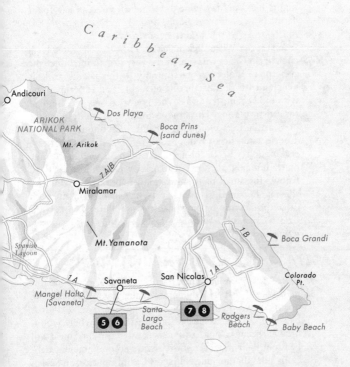

C a r i b b e a n   S e a

Andicouri

*ARIKOK
NATIONAL PARK*

Dos Playa

Boca Prins
(sand dunes)

Mt. Arikok

7 A/B

Miralamar

1 B

Boca Grandi

Mt. Yamanota

*Spanish
Lagoon*

1 A

Savaneta

San Nicolas

1 A

*Colorado
Pt.*

Mangel Halto
(Savaneta)

Santa
Largo
Beach

5 6

7 8

Rodgers
Beach

Baby Beach

KEY
Beaches

strawberries. ⑤ *Average main: $35* ✉ *California Lighthouse* ☎ *297/586–0786* ⊕ *www.faroblancorestaurant.com.*

$$$$ ✕ **The Restaurant at Tierra del Sol.** *International.* The main restaurant at Tierra del Sol sits next to the clifftop pool and golf course and offers great views of the northwest coast and the California lighthouse. The menu revolves around prime steaks, chops, and traditional fish and seafood with a nod to more exotic offerings like venison and Asian tuna. **Known for:** great views and romantic candlelight alfresco dining; popular a la carte Sunday brunch; special theme nights like Tuesday wine days and all-you-can-eat Tapas Thursdays. ⑤ *Average main: $40* ✉ *Tierra del Sol Resort* ☎ *297/586–7800* ⊕ *www.tierradelsol.com.*

★ Fodor'sChoice ✕ **White Modern Cuisine.** *Fusion.* Celebrated local
$$$$ chef Urvin Croes was one of the very first to introduce the concept of molecular gastronomy to this island, and his penchant for deconstructing elements and experimenting with food chemistry and flavors is rivaled only by his talent for artistic plating. This unique dining spot overlooking the pool at the luxe Gold Coast Estates Clubhouse provides a perfect setting of indoor and outdoor dining for those seeking to try his avant-garde creations as well as his take on traditional dishes like Aruban stew and Chilean sea bass. **Known for:** small-plates menu that encourages grazing and sharing; hoisin-glazed duck; prix-fixe surprise menu, with or without wine pairings. ⑤ *Average main: $40* ✉ *Gold Coast Estates, Diamante 300* ☎ *297/280–2800* ⊕ *www. whitecuisine.com.*

SANTA CRUZ AND THE INTERIOR

★ Fodor'sChoice ✕ **Casibari Cafe.** *Barbecue.* The bizarre rock for-
$$ mations at Casibari, which may make you feel as if you've dropped into the Flintstones's dining room, make a great backdrop to this casual, offbeat restaurant, where wood-fired barbecue is king. Your generously portioned meal will be fire-grilled under the stars, always accompanied by delicious sides that include cole slaw, Caribbean rice, and Casibari beans. **Known for:** completely alfresco atmosphere; hearty portions of grilled meats; cheap prices. ⑤ *Average main: $15* ✉ *Casabari Rocks, Paradera* ☎ *297/586–1775* ⊕ *www.casibaricafe.com* ⊘ *Closed Sun.*

Chowing Down Aruban Style

With its pristine white-sand beaches, clear blue waters, and near-perfect year-round weather, Aruba is a mecca for vacationers looking for a warm getaway. The island caters to the demanding tourism industry, which has resulted in a mainly resort-food scene. But if you're interested in tasting something other than standard American fare—and something a bit more unique to the Dutch- and Caribbean-influenced island—then you ought to try one of these local treats.

Balashi: After a day at the beach there's nothing better than sipping a nice, cold Balashi, Aruba's national beer and the only beer brewed on the island. The taste of Balashi is comparable to a Dutch pilsner.

Bitterballen: Crispy bite-size meatballs, which are breaded and then deep-fried, make for the perfect savory snack or appetizer. Dip them in a side of mustard, and wash them down with a cold beverage.

Keshi Yena: A traditional Aruban dish made with chicken, beef, or seafood in a rich brown sauce of spices and raisins, keshi yena is served with rice in a hollowed-out Gouda cheese rind.

Funchi: This classic Aruban cornmeal side dish is eaten at all times of day and is commonly served with soup.

Pan Bati: The slightly sweet pancakes are commonly eaten as a side with meat, fish, or soup entrées.

Pan Dushi: Delectable little raisin bread rolls are *dushi*, which is Papiamento for "sweet."

Pastechi: Aruba's favorite fast food is an empanadalike fried pastry filled with spiced meat, fish, or cheese.

Kesio: This popular dessert is essentially a custard flan or crème caramel.

Cocada: Bite-size pieces of these sweet coconut candies are typically served on a coconut shell.

SAVANETA

★ **Fodor's**Choice ✕ **Flying Fishbone.** *International.* Opened in 1977, **$$$$** this was the first restaurant in Aruba to offer feet-in-the-water dining, and that's why the legendary landmark is so worth the trek out to Savaneta for its insanely romantic seaside setting. An international menu is designed to please all palates, but the real culinary draw is fish straight from the island's most famous local fisherman's pier located a few doors over. **Known for:** "Savaneta's Seafood History" featuring the very local catch of the day; personal flambéed baked Alaska; tables set right in the ocean. ⑤ *Average main: $34* ⊠ *Savaneta 344, Savaneta* ☎ *297/584–2506* ⊕ *www.flyingfishbone.com.*

$ × **Zeerovers.** *Caribbean.* With a name that means "pirates"
FAMILY in Dutch, this small restaurant sits right on the Savaneta pier, where the local fishermen bring in their daily catch. The menu is basic: that day's fish and other seafood fried almost as soon as it's lifted out of the boat, with sides of local staples like plantains. **Known for:** freshest fish on the island; lively local hangout; picturesque sea view and sunsets. ⑤ *Average main: $10* ⊠ *Savaneta Pier, Savaneta* ☎ *297/584–8401* ⊘ *Closed Mon.* ⊟ *No credit cards.*

SAN NICOLAS

★ Fodor'sChoice × **Charlie's Restaurant & Bar.** *Caribbean.* Since
$$$ 1941, Charlie's Bar has been the heart and soul of San Nicolas, famous for its interior decorated with the eclectic detritus left behind by years of visitors. But it also serves surprisingly good food, including superb fresh fish and shrimp, as well as killer steaks. **Known for:** a legendary San Nicolas institution; "Boozer Coladas," the signature drink; third-generation owner named Charles. ⑤ *Average main: $25* ⊠ *Zeppenfeldstraat 56, San Nicolas* ☎ *297/584–5086* ⊘ *Closed Sun. No dinner Mon.–Wed. and Fri.–Sat.*

$$ × **O'Neil Caribbean Kitchen.** *Caribbean.* Right smack in the
FAMILY middle of the exciting new San Nicolas art walk, you'll find a warm and welcoming eatery, which is the ideal spot to get your Jamaican jerk on. You can also order real deal Jamaican dishes like ackee with salt fish and oxtail with beans, but the menu also has many local Aruban specialties like goat stew and fresh local fish and seafood. **Known for:** all-inclusive Sunday brunch buffet; real deal Jamaica specialties like ackee with salt fish; local favorite. ⑤ *Average main: $15* ⊠ *Bernard van de Veen Zeppenfeldstraat 15, San Nicolas* ☎ *297/584–8700* ⊘ *Monday.*

WHERE TO STAY

THERE'S A GOOD REASON WHY Aruba has one of the highest repeat-visitor ratios in the Caribbean (some 65% of all first-time visitors return): this island just does tourism right. Beyond the allure of the superb beaches and perfect year-round weather, the level of service and the standards of quality are very high.

Accommodations in Aruba run the gamut from large high-rise hotels and resorts to sprawling condo complexes to small, locally owned boutique establishments, and even luxury villa rentals in well-designed private communities where fractional ownership is also an option. Most hotels are west of Oranjestad, along L. G. Smith and J. E. Irausquin boulevards. Many are self-contained complexes, with restaurants, shops, casinos, water-sport centers, health clubs, and spas. And there are a surprising number of small and economical apartment-style hotels, bed-and-breakfasts, and family-run escapes in the interior if you know where to look. The number of all-inclusive options is growing, and increasingly, big-name-brand hotels are beginning to offer more comprehensive meal plan options. But these are still outnumbered by apartment rentals, which are many and varied all over the island. Savaneta now offers South Pacific over-the-water-style bungalows at Aruba Ocean Villas. Time-shares have always been big on this island, and the Divi family of resorts offers many different options in their various locations.

The Aruba Tourism Authority honors its repeat guests with a distinguished visitor Ambassador Program. Visitors of 10, 20, and 30 years running receive a certificate and get their photos in the newspaper as part of an appreciation ceremony.

ORGANIZATIONS

The Aruba Hotel & Tourism Association (better known as AHATA) was established in 1965 to maintain high standards in the tourism industry. From its original seven hotels, the organization has grown to more than 80 businesses, including restaurants, casinos, stores, tour operators, and airlines. The organization's budget, earmarked to promote Aruba as a travel destination, comes from a 9.5% room tax that funds both it and the newly privatized Aruba Tourism Authority. You can express opinions and register complaints on the Aruba Tourism website (⊕ *www.aruba. com*). The organization is also involved in anti-littering efforts as part of the Aruba Limpi Committee.

Contacts Aruba Hotel & Tourism Association. ☎ *297/582–2607* ⊕ *www.ahata.com.*

PRICES

Hotel rates are high; to save money, take advantage of airline and hotel packages, or visit in summer when rates are discounted by as much as 40%. If you're traveling with kids, ask about discounts; children often stay for free in their parents' room, though there are age cutoffs.

	WHAT IT COSTS IN U.S. DOLLARS			
	$	$$	$$$	$$$$
Hotels	under $275	$275–$375	$376–$475	over $475

Prices are for two people in a standard double room in high season, excluding 8% taxes and 11% service charges.

The following reviews have been condensed for this book. For expanded lodging reviews and current deals, visit Fodors.com.

TYPES OF LODGINGS

Almost all the resorts are along the island's southwest coast, along L. G. Smith and J. E. Irausquin boulevards, the larger high-rise properties being farther away from Oranjestad. A few budget places are in Oranjestad itself and in the interior around Noord and Bubali. Since most of Aruba's beaches are equally fabulous, it's the resort, rather than its location, that's going to be a bigger factor in how you enjoy your vacation.

Large Resorts: These all-encompassing vacation destinations offer myriad dining options, casinos, shops, water-sports centers, health clubs, and car-rental desks. The island also has many all-inclusive options.

Time-Shares: Large time-share properties are also popular, luring visitors who prefer to prepare some of their own meals and have a bit more living space than you might find in the typical resort hotel room.

Boutique Resorts: You'll find a few small resorts that offer more personal service, though not always with the same level of luxury as the larger places. But smaller resorts better reflect the natural sense of Aruban hospitality you'll find all over the island. There are some lovely B&Bs as well.

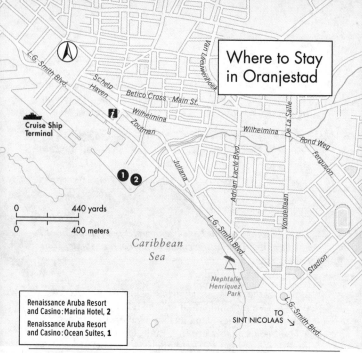

Renaissance Aruba Resort
and Casino: Marina Hotel, **2**

Renaissance Aruba Resort
and Casino: Ocean Suites, **1**

ORANJESTAD AND ENVIRONS

★ Fodor'sChoice 🍸 **Renaissance Aruba Resort and Casino: Marina**
$$$ Hotel. *Hotel.* Completely renovated in 2017, the adults-only
side of the Aruba Renaissance twin resorts offers guests
a chic, waterfront urban oasis in the heart of downtown
Oranjestad, including water taxi access to a luxurious
private island beach. **Pros:** near downtown shopping and
dining; good choice of in-hotel nightlife and restaurants;
beautiful private island beach with deluxe cabana rentals.
Cons: rooms are small and have no balconies; Marina pool is
tiny; nights can be noisy. 💲 *Rooms from: $390* ⊠ *L.G. Smith*
Blvd. 82, Oranjestad ☎ *297/583–6000, 800/421–8188*
⊕ *www.renaissancearuba.com* ⇱ *297 rooms* ⏇ *Breakfast.*

★ Fodor'sChoice 🍸 **Renaissance Aruba Resort and Casino: Ocean**
$$$ Suites. *Resort.* Part of the large Renaissance Aruba resort
FAMILY complex, the family-friendly sister of the Renaissance
Marina Hotel has its own man-made beach right on the
sea in the heart of downtown Oranjestad as well as spacious
suites with microwaves and mini-refrigerators; guests also
get access to the family-friendly side of the private island.
Pros: large and accommodating rooms; family-friendly luxe

The Renaissance Aruba's private island

cabana rentals at their private island; superb kid-friendly swimming on a man-made protected beach. **Cons:** meal plans available for longer stays, but little family-friendly dining on the property; very busy urban area; not all rooms have sea views. ⑤ *Rooms from: $389* ✉ *Renaissance Beach Oranjestad, L. G. Smith Blvd. 82, Oranjestad* ☎ *297/583–6000* ⊕ *www.renaissancearubaresortandcasino.com* ⤳ *259 rooms* ⑩ *Breakfast.*

DRUIF

$ **Aruba Beach Club.** *Hotel.* A favorite for families as well
FAMILY as those on a budget, Aruba Beach Club offers basic studios and one-bedroom units that attract repeat customers who enjoy a homey getaway on a great beach. **Pros:** family-friendly atmosphere; great beach; good value. **Cons:** pool area can be very busy; charge for Wi-Fi except at common area; service is uninspired except in the restaurant. ⑤ *Rooms from: $200* ✉ *J.E. Irausquin Blvd. 51–53, Punta Brabo* ☎ *297/582–3000* ⊕ *www.arubabeachclub.net* ⤳ *131 rooms* ⑩ *No meals.*

★ Fodor's Choice **Bucuti and Tara Beach Resort.** *Hotel.* The
$$$$ LEED-silver certified Bucuti is one of the greenest operating hotels in the Caribbean, but as the only adults-only luxury boutique hotel on Aruba, it's more famous for being one of the most romantic. **Pros:** spectacular pristine beach setting; free iPads and free Wi-Fi for guest use; accessible manage-

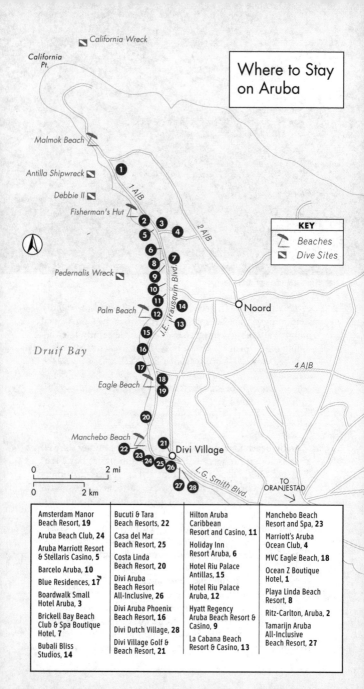

Where to Stay on Aruba

California Wreck

California Pt.

Malmok Beach

Antilla Shipwreck

Debbie II

Fisherman's Hut

Pedernalis Wreck

Palm Beach

Druif Bay

Eagle Beach

Manchebo Beach

1 A|B

2 A|B

J.E. Irausquin Blvd.

4 A|B

○ Noord

Divi Village

L.G. Smith Blvd.

TO ORANJESTAD

KEY

☂ *Beaches*

◣ *Dive Sites*

0 — 2 mi

0 — 2 km

Amsterdam Manor Beach Resort, **19**

Aruba Beach Club, **24**

Aruba Marriott Resort & Stellaris Casino, **5**

Barcelo Aruba, **10**

Blue Residences, **17**

Boardwalk Small Hotel Aruba, **3**

Brickell Bay Beach Club & Spa Boutique Hotel, **7**

Bubali Bliss Studios, **14**

Bucuti & Tara Beach Resorts, **22**

Casa del Mar Beach Resort, **25**

Costa Linda Beach Resort, **20**

Divi Aruba Beach Resort All-Inclusive, **26**

Divi Aruba Phoenix Beach Resort, **16**

Divi Dutch Village, **28**

Divi Village Golf & Beach Resort, **21**

Hilton Aruba Caribbean Resort and Casino, **11**

Holiday Inn Resort Aruba, **6**

Hotel Riu Palace Antillas, **15**

Hotel Riu Palace Aruba, **12**

Hyatt Regency Aruba Beach Resort & Casino, **9**

La Cabana Beach Resort & Casino, **13**

Manchebo Beach Resort and Spa, **23**

Marriott's Aruba Ocean Club, **4**

MVC Eagle Beach, **18**

Ocean Z Boutique Hotel, **1**

Playa Linda Beach Resort, **8**

Ritz-Carlton, Aruba, **2**

Tamarijn Aruba All-Inclusive Beach Resort, **27**

ment, with owners often on property. **Cons:** a little too quiet for some (no nighttime entertainment); not all rooms have sea views; no longer doing beach weddings. ⑤ *Rooms from: $507* ✉ *L.G. Smith Blvd. 55B, Druif* ☎ *297/583–1100* ⊕ *www.bucuti.com* ⇋ *104 rooms* ⦿ *Breakfast.*

$ ⌦ **Casa del Mar Beach Resort.** *Resort.* The one-and two-bed-
FAMILY room suites at this beachside time-share resort are quite comfortable though not overly luxe, but they come with fully equipped kitchens, and the resort, which sits on a stellar broad white-sand beach, offers a wide range of amenities like tennis courts and a gym and services like water sports and a kids' program. **Pros:** home-away-from-home feeling; great beach location; family-friendly. **Cons:** pool area can get crowded; rooms feel a bit dated; few quiet spots on property. ⑤ *Rooms from: $200* ✉ *L.G. Smith Blvd. 53, Punta Brabo* ☎ *297/582–7000* ⊕ *www.casadelmar-aruba. com* ⇋ *147 suites* ⦿ *No meals.*

★ **Fodor'sChoice** ⌦ **Divi Aruba Beach Resort All-Inclusive.** *Resort.*
$$$$ The more upscale choice of Divi's two Aruba all-inclusives,
FAMILY which share a gorgeous quarter-mile of Druif Beach, had a 60-room addition in 2016 that added some superluxe two-bedroom oceanfront suites with whirlpool tubs. **Pros:** on wonderful stretch of beach with family-friendly surf; kids under 12 stay free; cosmopolitan lively vibe. **Cons:** older rooms are small by modern standards; not all rooms have sea views; reservations mandatory for the more upscale restaurants. ⑤ *Rooms from: $507* ✉ *L.G. Smith Blvd. 93, Druif* ☎ *297/525–5200, 800/554–2008* ⊕ *www.diviaruba. com* ⇋ *269 rooms* ⦿ *All-inclusive* ⊂ *3 or 5-night min.*

$$$ ⌦ **Divi Dutch Village.** *Hotel.* Completely renovated from top
FAMILY to bottom in 2017, this all-suite resort behind the Divi Aruba all-inclusive features three redesigned freshwater pools (one with a new swim-up bar), a new restaurant, updated room interiors, and much more. **Pros:** beautiful beach is just steps away, and supermarkets are within walking distance; spacious suites fully equipped with modern appliances; new all-inclusive option. **Cons:** not directly on the beach; no ocean views from any rooms; very quiet. ⑤ *Rooms from: $384* ✉ *J. E. Irausquin Blvd. 47, Druif* ☎ *297/583–5000, 800/367–3484* ⊕ *www.dividutchvillage. com* ⇋ *123 rooms* ⦿ *No meals.*

$$ ⌦ **Divi Village Golf & Beach Resort.** *Resort.* This all-suite resort
FAMILY is surrounded by a 9-hole golf course across the street from beautiful Druif Beach where a complimentary shuttle service and dedicated loungers and palapas wait for guests. **Pros:** excellent golf course; spacious suites, some

The beachfront at Bucuti & Tara Beach Resorts.

with private Jacuzzis and grills; lush and lovely grounds with freshwater lagoons and wildlife. **Cons:** no suites have two beds, only one bed and a sleeper sofa; the resort is not beachfront; no ocean views. ⓢ *Rooms from: $348* ✉ *J.E. Irausquin Blvd. 93, Druif* ☎ *297/583–5000* ⊕ *www.divi-village.com* ➴ *250 suites* ⓞⓘ *All-inclusive* ⚲ *3-night min.*

$$ ☒ **Manchebo Beach Resort and Spa.** *Resort.* One of the original low-rise resorts on Aruba celebrated its 50th birthday in 2017, and it's still a little beachfront gem that has refreshed and reinvented itself as a dedicated health and wellness resort. **Pros:** on the island's broadest and most pristine white-sand beach; all-inclusive meal plans available; intimate and personal. **Cons:** rooms are on the small side; not much in way of entertainment; not all rooms have sea views. ⓢ *Rooms from: $365* ✉ *J. E. Irausquin Blvd. 55, Druif* ☎ *297/582–3444, 800/223–1108* ⊕ *www.manchebo.com* ➴ *72 rooms* ⓞⓘ *Breakfast.*

$$$$ ☒ **Tamarijn Aruba All-Inclusive Beach Resort.** *Resort.* One of
FAMILY Aruba's original and most popular family-friendly all-inclusives—and a sister resort to the Divi Aruba—spans a gorgeous quarter-mile stretch of Druif Beach and offers access to the entire shared complex of bars, restaurants, and services. **Pros:** complimentary shuttle service between all Divi resorts and the Alhambra casino; superb swimming conditions for all ages; all rooms are oceanfront. **Cons:** rooms are small by modern standards; no room service; advance reservations for all restaurants. ⓢ *Rooms from:*

$550 ✉ *J.E. Irausquin Blvd. 41, Punta Brabo* ☎ *297/594–7888, 800/554–2008* ⊕ *www.tamarijnaruba.com* ⇆ *236 rooms* ⎢⊙⎢ *All-inclusive* ☞ *3-night min.*

EAGLE BEACH

$$ 🖳 **Amsterdam Manor Beach Resort.** *Hotel.* Amsterdam Manor
FAMILY is an intimate, family-run hotel with a genuinely friendly staff, offering excellent value without too many frills. **Pros:** feels like a European village; friendly and helpful staff; all-inclusive option available. **Cons:** across the road from the beach; small pool; Jet Skis at beach can be noisy. ⑤ *Rooms from: $350* ✉ *J.E. Irausquin Blvd. 252, Eagle Beach* ☎ *297/527–1100, 800/932–2310* ⊕ *www.amsterdammanor.com* ⇆ *72 rooms* ⎢⊙⎢ *No meals.*

$$ 🖳 **Blue Residences.** *Hotel.* Bookended by Aruba's two most famous beaches (Eagle and Palm) on its own private manmade sandy strand right across the street, the Blue Residence Towers—three columns of condo hotel-style suites ranging from one to five bedrooms—offer epic unfettered views of the sea. **Pros:** full concierge services; all rooms have great sea views; lovely infinity pool looks out on the sea. **Cons:** not directly on the beach; far walk to shopping; little on-site entertainment. ⑤ *Rooms from: $297* ✉ *J. E. Irausquin Blvd. 26, Eagle Beach* ☎ *297/528–7000* ⊕ *www.bluearuba.com* ⇆ *120 room* ⎢⊙⎢ *No meals* ☞ *3-night min.*

$ 🖳 **Bubali Bliss Studios.** *Hotel.* Secreted behind Super Food, this economical option is within walking distance of famed Eagle Beach, with beautifully decorated rooms (all of which have modern kitchens) and an inviting oasis pool. **Pros:** flexible anytime self-check-in and check-out; pool garden area with hammocks; free Wi-Fi. **Cons:** front looks onto back door of a supermarket; 3-night minimum stay requirement; no on-site dining. ⑤ *Rooms from: $205* ✉ *Bubali 147 Eagle Beach, Eagle Beach* ☎ *297/587–5262* ⊕ *www.bubalibliss.com* ⇆ *10 rooms* ⎢⊙⎢ *No meals* ☞ *3-night min.*

$$ 🖳 **Costa Linda Beach Resort.** *Resort.* This all-suite, four-story,
FAMILY horseshoe-shaped time-share resort hugs a gorgeous 600-foot circle of beach and has a large pool and water circuit replete with whirlpools and fountains. **Pros:** spacious fully equipped suites; many activities available on-site; great beach. **Cons:** not all rooms have sea views; can get noisy when kids are everywhere; more expensive than some comparable properties in the area. ⑤ *Rooms from: $372* ✉ *J. E. Irausquin Blvd. 59, Eagle Beach* ☎ *297/583–8000* ⊕ *www.costalinda-aruba.com* ⇆ *155 rooms* ⎢⊙⎢ *No meals.*

5

DID YOU KNOW?

Hurricanes don't always cause beach erosion. When Hurricane Ivan passed north of Aruba in 2004 (one of the rare hurricanes that directly affected the island), Eagle Beach actually got a few feet wider.

Amsterdam Manor Beach Resort, a small hotel on Eagle Beach, is still family-run.

★ **Fodor's** Choice 🏨 **La Cabana Beach Resort & Casino.** *Resort.* A
$$ warm and friendly complex of mostly time-share units
FAMILY draws repeat visitors (primarily families), who enjoy the
spacious accommodations equipped with everything you
could possibly need for a home base away from home,
including a fully equipped kitchen. **Pros:** lively fami-
ly-friendly atmosphere with large pool facilites; the only
on-resort chapel on the island; laundry facilities on every
floor. **Cons:** you must cross the road to get to the beach;
limited number of shade palapas; few rooms have sea
views. $ *Rooms from: $246* ✉ *J.E. Irausquin Blvd. 250,
Eagle Beach* ☎ *520–1100* ⊕ *www.lacabana.com* ⇨ *449
rooms* ⦿ *Breakfast.*

$ 🏨 **MVC Eagle Beach.** *Hotel.* A tiny budget boutique hotel
across the road from a very quiet portion of beautiful
Eagle Beach, this is your best bet for a no-frills, clean and
comfortable stay at a good price. **Pros:** unbeatable price;
free Wi-Fi; friendly and helpful staff. **Cons:** lacks all the
amenities of larger resorts; not for those who want to
be away from children; across the street from the beach.
$ *Rooms from: $217* ✉ *J.E. Irausquin Blvd. 240, Eagle
Beach* ☎ *297/587–0110* ⊕ *www.mvceaglebeach.com* ⇨ *19
rooms* ⦿ *No meals.*

PALM BEACH AND NOORD

★ Fodor'sChoice ⌧ **Aruba Marriott Resort & Stellaris Casino.** *Resort.*
$$$$ This full-service resort offers both family-friendly ame-
FAMILY nities as well as an adults-only luxury floor with its own
pool and bar. **Pros:** inviting full-service spa and beauty
salon; calm, kid-friendly surf out front; one of the best
casinos on the islands. **Cons:** charge for in room Wi-Fi
beyond lobby and public areas; not all rooms have
sea views; beach can become crowded in high season.
⑤ *Rooms from: $589* ⌧ *L.G. Smith Blvd. 101, Palm Beach*
☎ *297/586–9000, 800/223–6388* ⊕ *www.marriott.com*
⇔ *414 rooms* ⋈ *No meals.*

$$$$ ⌧ **Barcelo Aruba.** *Resort.* On a stellar expanse of beachfront,
FAMILY this family-friendly all-inclusive offers something for everyone, with an extensive pool complex, great nightly entertainment, a dedicated kid's club, and an eclectic choice of à
la carte dining. **Pros:** spacious rooms, many with good sea
views; excellent location for Palm Beach water sports and
shopping; Royal Club level has a dedicated dining room and
lounge. **Cons:** beach can get very crowded; pool area can be
very noisy; charge for Wi-Fi beyond lobby. ⑤ *Rooms from:*
$600 ⌧ *J.E. Irausquin Blvd. 83, Palm Beach* ☎ *586–4500*
⊕ *www.barcelo.com* ⇔ *373 rooms* ⋈ *All-inclusive.*

★ Fodor'sChoice ⌧ **Boardwalk Small Hotel Aruba.** *Hotel.* A gor-
$$$ geous and luxurious boutique tropical oasis across the
road from Palm Beach, this family-run gem offers charming
casita-style rooms that surround an inviting pool. **Pros:**
beautiful grounds and decor; dedicated beach space with
chair service and shade palapas; highly personal service.
Cons: not right on the beach; no housekeeping or concierge
services on Sunday; no restaurant. ⑤ *Rooms from: $405*
⌧ *Bakval 20, Palm Beach* ☎ *297/586–6654* ⊕ *www.board-*
walkaruba.com ⇔ *14 rooms* ⋈ *No meals.*

$ ⌧ **Brickell Bay Beach Club & Spa Boutique Hotel.** *Hotel.* Right
in the heart of the main tourist street behind the high-rise
resort Palm Beach strip is this adults-only urban stay with
its own hidden pool and courtyard. **Pros:** resort has a small
spa on-site; free Wi-Fi and calls to North America; dedi-
cated space on Palm Beach with free shuttle. **Cons:** noisy,
busy area; no ocean views; busy pool. ⑤ *Rooms from: $225*
⌧ *J. E. Irausquin Blvd. 370, Palm Beach* ☎ *297/586–0900*
⊕ *www.brickellbayaruba.com* ⇔ *98 rooms* ⋈ *Breakfast.*

5

The Aruba Marriott Resort & Stellaris Casino is in the heart of Palm Beach.

★ **Fodor's**Choice ⛱ **Divi Aruba Phoenix Beach Resort.** *Resort.* With
$$$$ incredible views from its high-rise tower, stunning rooms
FAMILY awash in tropical colors and state-of–the-art amenities, and
comfortable, homey accommodations, Divi Aruba Phoenix
rises above the fray on busy Palm Beach. **Pros:** beautifully
appointed rooms, some with whirlpool bathtubs; great
private beach away from the main Palm Beach frenzy;
all units have sea views. **Cons:** no shuttle service to other
Divi properties; no all-inclusive plan; no reserving shade
palapas. ⑤ *Rooms from: $636* ✉ *J.E. Irausquin Blvd. 75,
Palm Beach* ☎ *297/586–1170* ⊕ *www.diviarubaphoenix.
com* ☞ *240 rooms* ⎪◎⎪ *Breakfast.*

$$$$ ⛱ **Hilton Aruba Caribbean Resort and Casino.** *Hotel.* After a
FAMILY complete renovation in late 2016, the landmark Radisson
became a Hilton but may still be recognizable to some
from the hotel layout and the 15 iconic acres of tropical
gardens and extensive pool area just off busy Palm Beach.
Pros: excellent beachfront spa; modern look and feel; lots
of entertainment and activities for families. **Cons:** not all
rooms have sea views; long lines at the breakfast buffets;
on-site food and drink is pricey. ⑤ *Rooms from: $599* ✉ *J.E.
Irausquin Blvd. 81, Palm Beach* ☎ *297/586–6555* ⊕ *www3.
hilton.com* ☞ *357 rooms* ⎪◎⎪ *No meals.*

$$ ⛱ **Holiday Inn Resort Aruba.** *Resort.* The resort's massive lem-
FAMILY on-yellow buildings that sprawl across a prime spot on Palm
Beach offer a revelation compared to what most might think
a Holiday Inn stay might entail, offering inviting rooms, a

fun vibe and distinct sections that will appeal to those looking for quiet active fun, or a family-friendly environment.
Pros: thematic zones provide distinct amenities; kids eat
and stay free and enjoy an excellent stand-alone kid's club;
excellent on-site dining can include an all-inclusive meal
plan. **Cons:** not all rooms have sea views; the casino (not
owned by the resort) needs updating; reception is frequently
busy with big groups. *⑤Rooms from: $325 ⊠ J.E. Irausquin
Blvd. 230, Palm Beach ☎ 297/586–3600, 800/465–4329
⊕ www.holidayarubaresort.com ⇋ 603 rooms ⏀ No meals.*

$$$ ⬚ **Hotel Riu Palace Antillas.** *Resort.* Right next door to its
family-friendly sister, this high-rise tower (once the Westin)
is strictly for adults, offering all-inclusive rates and a fabu-
lous pool area as well as stellar sea views from many rooms.
Pros: full bottles of standard spirits, beer, and soft drinks in
all rooms; arguably the best and biggest all-inclusive buffet on
the island; 24/7 room service included. **Cons:** rooms are small
by modern standards; common areas appear more corporate
than resort-tropical; not all rooms have a sea view. *⑤Rooms
from: $ 405 ⊠ J.E. Irausquin Blvd. 77, Palm Beach ☎ 297/
526–4100 ⊕ www.riu.com ⇋ 481 rooms ⏀ All-inclusive.*

$$ ⬚ **Hotel Riu Palace Aruba.** *Resort.* This family-friendly all-in-
FAMILY   clusive is a massive complex surrounding an expansive
water circuit leading to the sea with a choice of five restaurants and offering scads of free activities. **Pros:** spacious
water circuit for families; a wide choice of entertainment
and dining; nice shallow beachfront. **Cons:** beach and pool
area get very busy and noisy; few spots to escape in soli-
tiude; few rooms have unobstructed sea views. *⑤Rooms
from: $325 ⊠ J.E. Irausquin Blvd. 79, Palm Beach ☎ 297/
586–3900 ⊕ www.riu.com ⇋ 400 rooms ⏀ All-inclusive.*

$$$$ ⬚ **Hyatt Regency Aruba Beach Resort & Casino.** *Resort.* This
12-acre property is one of the most lavishly landscaped
resorts on the island, with a glorious array of bright tropical
blooms and lush foliage surrounding a circuit of waterfalls
culminating in a koi pond where black swans glide grace-
fully by. **Pros:** beautiful grounds; great for kids; excellent
restaurants. **Cons:** small balconies for a luxury hotel; some
rooms are quite a stretch from the beach; not all rooms
have sea views. *⑤Rooms from: $650 ⊠ J.E. Irausquin Blvd.
85, Palm Beach ☎ 297/586–1234, 800/554–9288 ⊕ aruba.
hyatt.com ⇋ 395 rooms ⏀ Breakfast.*

$$$$ ⬚ **Marriott's Aruba Ocean Club.** *Rental.* First-rate amenities
FAMILY   and lavishly decorated villas with balconies and full kitchens have made this time-share an island favorite. **Pros:**
relaxed atmosphere; feels more like a home than a hotel

5

room; excellent beach. **Cons:** beach can get crowded; attracts large families, so lots of kids are about; grounds are not in sea view. ⑤ *Rooms from: $650* ✉ *L.G. Smith Blvd. 99, Palm Beach* ☎ *297/586–2641* ⊕ *www.marriott. com* ⮞ *206 rooms* ⦿ *No meals.*

$$ ☷ **Playa Linda Beach Resort.** *Resort.* Looking something like a
FAMILY stepped Mayan pyramid—the design maximizes sea views from the balconies—this older time-share hotel also has a homey feel, with full kitchens in all the spacious units. **Pros:** great beach location; spacious rooms; lots of distractions for the kids. **Cons:** not all rooms are of the same standard; crowded and busy beachfront; furnishings are dated. ⑤ *Rooms from: $325* ✉ *J. E. Irausquin Blvd. 87, Palm Beach* ☎ *297/586–1000* ⊕ *www.playalinda.com* ⮞ *144 rooms* ⦿ *No meals.*

$$$$ ☷ **Ritz-Carlton, Aruba.** *Hotel.* Bookending the long string of resorts along famed Palm Beach, this massive hotel sits on a broad stretch of white sand with all rooms overlooking the sea. **Pros:** exemplary personal service including beach servers on Segways; spacious grounds so it never feels crowded; stunning sunset views from all rooms and the two-story atrium lobby bar. **Cons:** sheer size and design gives it a big-box feel; attracts many large groups; pricey for standard rooms compared to others of similar quality on the same beach. ⑤ *Rooms from: $799* ✉ *Palm Beach, L.G. Smith Blvd. 107, Palm Beach* ☎ *527–2222* ⊕ *www.ritz-carlton.com/en/hotels/caribbean/aruba* ⮞ *320* ⦿ *No meals.*

WESTERN TIP

  ★ Fodor'sChoice ☷ **Ocean Z Boutique Hotel.** *Hotel.* A unique luxury
$$$$ boutique resort far from the touristy fray is across the road from the wild and scenic Malmok Cliffs, offering rooms surrounding a solarium pool as well as a few oceanfront suites. **Pros:** chic solitary escape away from the crowds; georgeous scenic setting with sea views; intimate and personal first-rate service. **Cons:** not within walking distance to any other dining or shopping; is not on a beach; no entertainment. ⑤ *Rooms from: $490* ✉ *L.G. Smith Blvd. 526, Malmokweg* ☎ *297/586–9500* ⊕ *www.oceanzaruba. com* ⮞ *13 rooms* ⦿ *Breakfast.*

NIGHTLIFE AND PERFORMING ARTS

YOU'LL NEVER NEED TO WAIT until the sun goes down on Aruba to get the party started. The revelry starts early at beach bars and resort happy hours where live music or DJ-driven sounds shake the sunbathers out of their tropical relaxation mode and into barefoot-bopping in the sand. And chances are good on any given week that there will be some kind of day party happening because of one of the many celebrations this island has going on all year long. There are about 50-some annual events—carnivals, regattas, sporting competitions, national holiday fêtes, seasonal celebrations, and music, food, wine, and art festivals each year—so whenever you visit, there's bound to be some daytime fun and dancing in the streets or on the beaches.

But once the moon rises and the tiki torches are lighted, you will notice a shift in mood from happy party time to high-octane energy. And if you follow the sounds of music along the high-rise strip or in downtown Oranjestad, you're bound to find a happening that suits your style, be it kicking back in a cozy lounge or dancing until dawn. You can easily hop from scene to scene on foot in both places, or take a barhopping bus to discover where the nights really move, along with a wild and crazy crowd. Taxis are easy to find, and the party scene is compact, so there is no need to wander far.

NIGHTLIFE

For information on specific events, check out the free magazines *Aruba Nights, Aruba Experience,* and *Island Temptations,* all available at the airport and at hotels.

TOURS

★ Fodor'sChoice **Kukoo Kunuku Party Bus & Wine and Tapas Tours.**
Aruba's premier wild and crazy party bus outfit has been operating since the late 1990s, and they've added a new twist. By night, it's all about shaking your maracas and barhopping through the town via their famous Pub Krawl tour, or doing a dinner and barhop night that stops at the cool Casibari Grill in the outback for great barbecue and then motors on for a wild tour to local party spots. But you now have a more elegant and low-key option that begins early and takes you to some of the island's best dining spots for wine and tapas. It's called Wine On Down The Road, and it's a great way to preview some of Aruba's top culinary gems before you commit to a night out. A pro-

Oranjestad Renaissance

Aruba's historic port capital city Oranjestad has always had a colorful Dutch colonial charm, but the past few years have seen a major face-lift and renewal throughout downtown to better accommodate a growing local population and better welcome the million-plus visitors it sees each year. To make the cruise terminal more inviting and the first impression of the city more alluring, all cargo traffic operations have been moved to Barcadera. Some back streets have been closed to traffic, making new pedestrian malls and courtyards that allow visitors to wander past the harbor village and back into the original Main Street (G. F. Betico Croes) area that is two streets behind the harbor. A new free eco-trolley makes it easy to explore all corners of the newly refreshed downtown, starting at the cruise terminal and looping throughout the shops, attractions, museums, dining spots, and malls, and reaching right to the public bus terminal. Visitors can hop on and off at will; it travels very slowly so you can get a good look at what's on offer. The recent Oranjestad renaissance has been well received, bringing new businesses and attractions and kicking off a good start to the continuing construction of a new Linear Park that will connect downtown to the main tourist beaches by boardwalk and when completed will become the longest park of its kind in the Caribbean. Phase 1, which connects Oranjestad to the airport by a paved trail, is complete.

fessional sommelier joins to inform guests about the wine pairings. Hotel pickup and drop-off are always included, but there are no tours on Sundays. ⊠ *Noord 128 P, Noord* ☎ *297/586–2010* ⊕ *www.kukookunuku.com* 🎫 *From $46.*

WEEKLY PARTIES

★ **Fodor's Choice Bon Bini Festival.** This year-round folklore event (the name means "welcome" in Papiamento), is held every Tuesday from 6:30 pm to 8:30 pm at Ft. Zoutman in Oranjestad. In the inner courtyard, you can check out the Antillean dancers in resplendent costumes, feel the rhythms of the steel drums, browse among the stands displaying local artwork, and sample local food and drink. ⊠ *Fort Zoutman, Oranjestad* ⊕ *www.aruba.com* 🎫 *$5.*

San Nicolas Carubbian Festival. Every Thursday night in San Nicolas, the main streets of Aruba's old refinery town that locals called Sunrise City come to life in a spectacular fashion with a minicarnival called the Carubbian Festival. It's a culture and heritage extravaganza featuring live music, dance performances, and even a big colorful parade finale, where visitors are encouraged to fully participate. There are also arts and crafts stalls and food and drink kiosks set up for the occasion that offer local specialties. There are activities planned for children as well. Festival runs from 6 pm to 10 pm. Sometimes it takes a break the last weeks of December for the Christmas holidays and resumes in mid-January. ◼TIP➔ A hotel bus package is a good idea as the roads at night are not well lit, and navigation can be challenging. ✉ *Main St., San Nicolas* 🏷 *Free.*

ORANJESTAD AND ENVIRONS

Businesses come and go in the alfresco Renaissance Marketplace on the marina across from the Seaport Casino, but it's always a lively hot spot after the dinner hour, when most of the cafés, bistros, and restaurants transform the vibe with their own live music or entertainment. The sparkling lights on the water and the live bands playing in the common square every evening also add to the magic. Spots like Cuba's Cookin, Sidebar, Café the Plaza, and others often have special events. This is also the spot where pop-up festivals will be found at night. It's a popular gathering spot for locals as well as visitors.

★ Fodor'sChoice **Alfie's in Aruba.** Two Canadians bought this newly popular watering hole but they haven't forgotten their homeland; you can enjoy Canadian Moosehead beer and authentic Quebec-style poutine here just as easily as a Heinken or Corona. Also on tap are mega-burgers, Thursday rib nights, and live music every Friday. And of course, you can watch hockey. Look for the giant Canadian flag outside. It's closed on Mondays. ✉ *Dominicanessenstraat 10, Oranjestad* ☎ *297/569–5815* ⊕ *www.alfiesinaruba.com.*

★ Fodor'sChoice **BLUE.** Located steps away from the cool infinity pool of the Renaissance Marina Hotel, BLUE is one of the hippest social gathering spots on the island. It's the place where young local professionals gather for happy hour during the week. Later it morphs into a hot, nightly DJ-driven scene bathed in blue and violet lights with a giant video wall and talented barkeeps serving upscale concoc-

A sunset happy-hour cruise is a popular pastime.

tions like their signature Blue Solo Martini. Live bands and special shows are held monthly. ✉ *Renaissance Marina Hotel, L. G. Smith Blvd. 82, Oranjestad* ☎ *297/523–6115* ⊕ *www.renaissancearubaresortandcasino.com.*

Cafe Chaos. This is not so much a "dance club" as a place to dance and let loose for mostly local Dutch expats. The no-nonsense bar offers a wide variety of music, from live bands to DJs spanning styles from reggae to funk to rock. It's a mix, and it all depends on the mood of the crowd and the night. But it's a great spot to make new local friends. The live music often starts very late, but you can happen on some crazy jam sessions, too. ✉ *L.G. Smith Blvd. 60, Oranjestad* ☎ *297/588–7547.*

★ Fodor's Choice **Eetcafe The Paddock.** It's impossible to miss the big red roof just off the marina, especially since there is a large Holstein cow, a big dinosaur, and an entire car sitting on top of it! But that's the point. Wild, crazy, and whimsical is their claim to fame, and there's no better spot in town to catch Dutch "futball" if you're seeking the craziest orange-clad die-hard fans. Though it's a popular tourist lunch spot during the day, this joint really morphs into party-hearty mode at night, full of carousing locals and visitors alike enjoying the great deals on drinks via the late-night happy hours and dollar-beer specials. Live music often adds to the revelry. ✉ *L. G. Smith Blvd. 13, Oranjestad* ⊕ *www. paddock-aruba.com.*

The West Deck Island Grill Beach Bar. Just over the wooden walkway from Renaissance Ocean Suites along the Linear Park you'll find this casual wooden deck beach bar on the water that's called Governor's Bay. Enjoy one of their special upside-down margaritas or incredible craft cocktails while you catch a stellar sunset and watch the cruise ships go by. After dark, the music takes it up a notch—sometimes live—and the atmosphere is fun and friendly. It's as popular with locals as it is with visitors. Great Caribbean tapas and grilled specialties are also on tap. ⊠ *Governor's Bay Oranjestad, L.G. Smith Blvd.* ✣ *Linear Park (next to The Queen Wilhelmina Park-adjacent to The Renaissance Suites)* ☎ 587–2667 ⊕ *www.thewestdeck.com.*

7 West Bar & Restaurant. Named after its address (Westraat 7) this is predominantly an eatery for lunch and casual dinner in the early evening until the lights dim later on to reveal a seriously cool neon glow-in-the-dark interior that attracts a local crowd of thirsty folks seeking signature cocktails amid hot music in downtown Oranjestad. The deck overlooks the harbor. ⊠ *Weststraat 7, Oranjestad* ☎ 297/588–9983 ⊕ *www.7-westaruba.com.*

DRUIF

★ Fodor'sChoice **Fusions Wine and Tapas Piano Bar.** This classy lounge in the Alhambra Mall is an ideal spot to grab a glass of wine, a tasty bite, or a steak. There's usually soft, live piano music and a solo singer. Patrons are often stopping by before or after gambling at the big casino next door. Fusions is owned by the Divi group, so guests at those resorts should check with their concierge for special savings. ⊠ *Alhambra Mall, Druif* ☎ 297/280–9994 ⊕ *www.diviaruba.com/fusion-restaurant.htm.*

EAGLE BEACH

★ Fodor'sChoice **Heart Music Bar.** You can't miss the arty, colorful building with the giant heart on it—the new hot spot for young, hip locals to let loose and burn up the dance floor to house, techno, and EDM from Wednesday through Sunday. The building also houses a radio station (106.7 FM) that broadcasts the nightly revelry live. There are both inside and outdoor sections. Expect a lot of specials and good prices for drinks. ⊠ *Corral Mall, Taratata 15, Eagle Beach* ✣ *On the road between Eagle and Manchebo beaches* ☎ 297/593–4493 ⊕ *www.heartmusicbar.com.*

CLOSE UP

Brewing Up Something Special

Order a "Balashi cocktail" in Aruba only if you want to receive a glass of water. That's because the water purification plant is in Balashi. And don't be afraid to drink the water: it's safe and delicious and made from desalinated seawater. But since the advent of the beer called Balashi—the only beer in the world made from desalinated seawater—you might confuse a barkeep if you order just a "Balashi." The brewery has regularly scheduled tours should you want to see how it's made, and they also have a great beer garden and lunch spot. They are making more types of beer there now beyond their second offering, Balashi Chill, which is best enjoyed with a wedge of lime in the neck like many Mexican beers. Hopi Bon and Hopi Stout are the latest beer brews. (*Hopi Bon* means very good in Papiamento.)

PALM BEACH AND NOORD

6

The two-mile stretch of road in front of the high-rise resorts called The Strip is where you'll find most of the nightlife action in Palm Beach, though there are also some pubs and clubs worth seeking out in the surrounding areas of Noord. The clubs tend to come and go, but The Strip is always chock-full of opportunities to let loose after the sun goes down in the area's squares, courtyards, and outdoor malls, and threaded throughout are vendor kiosks. You can easily barhop on foot to find the vibe that suits you best by following the music that suits you best. If you're staying in a Palm Beach resort, there's no need for a car or taxi.

★ **Fodor'sChoice Bugaloe Bar & Grill.** Night and day, this crazy colorful beach bar at the tip of De Palm Pier on busy Palm Beach is hopping and bopping with visitors and locals alike. Paint-spattered wooden tables and chairs on a plank floor under a massive palapa draw barefoot beachcombers in for frozen cocktails, cold beer, and casual fare where live music is king. The revelry starts as early as happy hour and continues well into the evening. Karaoke nights, salsa nights, and even a crazy fish night on Mondays: there's always something wild and fun going on there. It's also an optimal spot to catch a magical sunset over the waves. There's free Wi-Fi, too. ⊠ *De Palm Pier, J. E. Irausquin Blvd. 79, De Palm Pier, Palm Beach* ☎ *297/586–2233* ⊕ *www.bugaloe.com.*

Café Rembrandt. Great schnitzels, hearty fare, and really low prices on cold imported beer and drinks bring the Dutch expats here in droves; everyone stays longer for the great camaraderie, twice-nightly happy hours, and the warm and friendly staff. There's occasional live music, and sometimes dancing on weekends. ⊠ *South Beach Centre, Palm Beach* ☎ *297/586–4747* ⊗ *Closed Mon.*

The Great Room Lobby Bar. Easy-listening local bands get the party started at the Aruba Marriott's newly renovated lobby bar. It's a classy venue and an ideal spot for before- or after-dinner drinks. And the bartenders take their creative mixology seriously, even competing in bartending competitions. Superb signature cocktails are what you come for. ⊠ *Aruba Marriott Resort & Stellaris Casino, L.G. Smith Blvd. 101, Palm Beach* ☎ *297/586–9000* ⊕ *www.marriott.com.*

★ **Fodor'sChoice Gusto.** Definitely Aruba's most cosmopolitan high-octane dance club, Gusto is where master bartenders show off excellent flair skills while serving up fabulous cocktails to pretty people who want to party late into the night. The island's hottest DJs and a dazzling light show keep the dancing going nonstop. Late-night happy hour is from 9 pm to 11 pm. All kinds of special events and theme nights add to Gusto's allure as a highly popular party spot. VIP bottle service is available, too. ⊠ *J.E. Irausquin Blvd. 348-A, Palm Beach* ☎ *297/592–8772* ⊗ *Closed Mon.*

★ **Fodor'sChoice Hard Rock Cafe Aruba.** This classic rock–branded bar and restaurant has anchored the nightlife scene along The Strip since 2008. You'll find live bands on a big outdoor stage cresting a massive terrace. You can come for a burger or the other hearty fare or just stand and enjoy the show. ⊠ *South Beach Building, Palm Beach 55, Palm Beach* ☎ *297/586–9986* ⊕ *www.hardrock.com.*

★ **Fodor'sChoice Legends Pub.** A truly American-style pub with a no-nonsense approach to getting folks to sleuth out their gray and glass building—way behind the Hyatt's parking lot—that looks more like an office building than a bar. They have succeeded in attracting crowds through word-of-mouth about their fab pub grub, great drinks, good prices, and super staff. Being a permanent home to NFL games doesn't hurt either. Locals and visitors alike enjoy the camaraderie, live music on their big terrace, special events like trivia nights, taco Tuesdays, wing Wednesdays, and hearty mains like prime rib. Flights of craft beer are also a specialty. ⊠ *L.G. Smith Blvd. 388, Palm Beach* ☎ *280–3330* ⊕ *www.legendspubaruba.com.*

CLOSE UP

Cool Concoctions

Aruba's skilled staff is, on the most part, far more than barkeeps—many are master mixologists who have trained in well-accredited institutions on-island and abroad. And they also often compete in international competitions. So before ordering a tried-and-true tropical favorite like a pina colada or the Island's best-known drink, the Aruba Ariba, bring a smile to their face by asking them to make you one of their original concoctions or a signature cocktail from the establishment's own bar menu. The taste and creativity is sure to bring a smile to you, too, and many of the specials are handcrafted with homegrown ingredients and artisanal liquors. And even if it's not the Christmas season, do seek out a sample of *ponche crema*—Aruba's extremely liquor-laden and beautifully spiced eggnog that's available all year-round and in take-home bottles. Also look for *coecoei*, a unique Aruban liqueur that tastes like anisette but is thicker and ruby red in color. It colors many island drinks instead of grenadine and is also good on its own on the rocks.

Local Store. Contrary to its name, it's not a store but a bar, and a very local one at that. Live local bands, lots of resident partiers, and a laid-back, down-to-earth atmosphere makes this the place to kick back and have fun, especially on weekends. Good prices on drinks, local beer, craft beers, and local Aruban snacks like funchi fries and over a dozen kinds of artisanal chicken wings attract the tourists, too. ⊠ *Palm Beach 13A, Noord* ☎ *297/586–1414* ⊕ *www.localstorearuba.com.*

★ FodorśChoice **MooMba Beach Bar.** As the central party spot on the busiest part of Palm Beach, this open-air bar is famous for its Sunday-night blowouts with big crowds of locals gathering to dance in the sand to live bands or DJs. The barkeeps are flair and mixology masters, and happy hours are very hot. You'll find both early and late drink specials every night except Sunday. The attached restaurant is also a wonderful surf-side spot for breakfast, lunch, and dinner. There's free Wi-Fi. ⊠ *J.E. Irausquin Blvd. 230, Palm Beach* ✛ *Between Holiday Inn and Marriott Surf Club* ☎ *297/586–5365* ⊕ *www.moombabeach.com.*

★ FodorśChoice **Pure Beach.** South Beach–style cocktails and tapas are served in this bar and restaurant in the Divi Phoenix Aruba Resort. It's got a cool, hip vibe, offering couches in the sand surf-side, which are lit by tiki torches at night; some kind of live music is often on the menu, too. It's an ideal place to kick off the night for a sunset happy hour cocktail or snack. ⊠ *Divi Phoenix Aruba Resort, J.E. Irausquin Blvd. 75, Palm Beach* ☎ *297/586–6606* ⊕ *www. purebeacharuba.com.*

★ Fodor'sChoice **Sopranos Piano Bar.** With a theme loosely based on the famous HBO series, Sopranos has a fun atmosphere, and live piano nightly encourages the crowd to join in a sing-along. Top-notch barkeeps shake up a big list of creative cocktails, including the famous signature Badabing Martini. An extensive wine and champane list will provide an option for those not obsessed with cocktails. And you can enjoy Cuban cigars on the outdoor terrace. A DJ sometimes plays late into the night on weekends. ⊠ *Arawak Garden Mall, L. G. Smith Blvd. 177, Palm Beach* ☎ *297/586–8622* ⊕ *www.sopranospianobararuba.com.*

PERFORMING ARTS

Aruba has a handful of not-so-famous but very talented performers. Over the years, several local artists, including composer Julio Renado Euson, choreographer Wilma Kuiperi, sculptor Ciro Abath, and visual artist Elvis Lopez, have gained international renown. Furthermore, many Aruban musicians play more than one type of music (classical, jazz, soca, salsa, reggae, calypso, rap, pop), and many compose as well as perform. Edjean Semeleer has followed in the footsteps of his mentor Padu Lampe—the composer of the island's national anthem and a beloved local star—to become one of the island's best-loved entertainers. His performances pack Aruba's biggest halls, especially his annual Christmas concert. He sings in many languages, and though he's young, his style is old-style crooner—Aruba's answer to Michael Bublé.

Cas Di Cultura. The National Theater of Aruba, the island's cultural center, hosts art exhibits, folkloric shows, dance performances, and concerts throughout the year. ⊠ *Vondellaan 2, Oranjestad* ☎ *297/582–1010* ⊕ *www.casdicultura.aw.*

★ Fodor'sChoice **UNOCA.** Although UNOCA is Aruba's national gallery, it's much more, acting as an anchor to host cultural and performance events, which are often held here. ⊠ *Stadionweg 21, Oranjestad* ☎ *297/583–5681* ⊕ *www. unocaaruba.org.*

Carnival

Aruba's biggest bash incorporates local traditions with those of Venezuela, Brazil, Holland, and North America. Trinidadians who came to work at the oil refinery in the 1940s introduced Carnival to the island, so it's only fitting that the new Carnival Village, Workshop and Museum was built in San Nicolas, where it all began. Though the town they call Sunrise City has always been the location for Carnival's Jouvert Morning Jump-Up (also called the Pajama Party, since it begins at 4 am and many people come straight from bed), most of the festivities have been held in Oranjestad over the years. Now the monthlong celebration swings more between the two towns with pageants,

parades, musical competitions, ceremonies, and gala concerts in both. But the Grand Parade held on the Sunday before Ash Wednesday still takes over all of downtown Oranjestad with thousands dancing in the streets and viewing the floats, costumes, and bands. All events end on Shrove Tuesday: at midnight an effigy of King Momo (traditionally depicted as a fat man) is burned, indicating the end of joy and the beginning of Lenten penitence. You can get a taste of the Carnival spirit every Thursday night in San Nicolas with the Carubbian Festival held year-round. Many hotels offer round-trip bus transportation and food and drink packages if you don't want to drive that far at night.

ANNUAL ARTS FESTIVALS

Finally, the island's many festivals showcase arts and culture. To find out what's going on, check out the local English-language newspapers or look for events online at aruba.com.

★ Fodor's Choice **Caribbean Sea Jazz Festival.** The music begins at intimate venues around the island and leads up to a big two-day jazz, soul, and Latin music festival held at the Renaissance Marketplace, usually in the third week of September. Big-name bands draw big crowds to the harbor, and the outdoor party continues long into the night all around Oranjestad with makeshift food stands and temporary bars. There is also a big on-site art event during the fest. ⊠ *Renaissance Marketplace, Oranjestad* ⊕ *www.caribbeanseajazz.com.*

The Dande Festival. Aruba's New Year traditions begin with a big bang before the big day, when Arubans light *pagaras*—

strings of hundreds of firecrackers—all over the island to celebrate a good year and chase out bad vibes. New Year's Eve sees the traditional islandwide fireworks, but they also usher in the New Year with Dande music. It used to be a "stroll" with groups of musicians going from house to house singing good-luck greetings right after midnight, but now it has become a bona-fide organized festival held with big groups competing for prizes during the week between Christmas and New Years Day. *Dande* comes from the Papiamento word *dandara,* which means "to have a good time." ⊕ *www.aruba.com/things-to-do/dande-festival.*

Dera Gai (*St. John's Day*). The annual harvest feast and "burying of the rooster" (*dera gai*) tradition is celebrated June 24 (the feast of St. John the Baptist). Festive songs, bright yellow-and-red costumes, and traditional dances mark this holiday dating from 1862. Today, the live rooster—which symbolizes a successful harvest—has been replaced by a plastic one. You will also notice smoke all around the island from the ceremonial bonfires traditionally lighted that day. ⊕ *www.aruba.com/things-to-do/dera-gai-st-johns-day.*

★ FodorsChoice **Soul Beach Festival.** This big festival is the island's top musical event. Held over May's Memorial Day weekend each year with the main events in downtown Oranjestad Harbor, it attracts big-name artists and huge crowds with smaller shows rotating locations all around the island. There are also comedy shows, a Soul Beach Fitness Challenge, and related pop-up parties galore islandwide. ⊕ *www. soulbeach.net.*

CASINOS

AMONG THE BIGGEST DRAWS IN Aruba are the island's elaborate, pulsating casinos. Aruba offers up gambling venues closer in spirit and form to Las Vegas than any other island in the Caribbean. Perhaps it's the predominantly American crowd, but the casinos remain busy and popular, and almost every big resort has one. Although people don't dress up as elegantly as they did in years gone by, most of the casinos still expect a somewhat more put-together look (in the evening, at least) than a T-shirt and flip-flops.

Aruba's casinos attract high rollers, low-stakes bettors, and nongamblers alike, and the island is the birthplace of Caribbean stud poker. Games include slot machines and blackjack (both beloved by North Americans), baccarat (preferred by South Americans), craps, roulette—even betting on sports events. Restaurants and bars have added another dimension to the casinos; some of these venus offer live music, and most casinos will serve you free drinks while you play. Almost all casinos have a player's club where you can sign up for a free account (passport or driver's license required) for the ability to earn complimentary match-and-play coupon or free play on slots. Many casinos feature afternoon bingo with big prizes (some of these games draw many locals as well). Few stay open all night, but most are open until at least 3 or 4 am. Look in the local magazines and guides for coupons for free play or match-and-play offers.

GAMBLING PRIMER

For a short-form handbook on the rules, the odds, and the strategies for the most popular casino games—or for help deciding on the kind of action that suits your style—read on.

THE GOOD BETS

The first part of any viable casino strategy is to risk the most money on wagers that present the lowest edge for the house. Blackjack, craps, video poker, and baccarat are the most advantageous to the bettor in this regard. The two types of bets at baccarat have a house advantage of a little more than 1%. The basic line bets at craps, if backed up with full odds, can be as low as 0.5%. Blackjack and video poker, at times, have a house edge that's less than 1% (nearly a 50–50 proposition), and with bettor diligence can actually present a slight long-term advantage.

The vibrant casino at the Ritz Carlton

How can a casino possibly provide you with a potentially positive expectation at some of its games? First, because a vast number of gamblers make the bad bets (those with a house advantage of 5%–35%, such as roulette, keno, and slots) day in and day out. Second, because the casino knows that very few people are aware of the opportunities to beat the odds. Third, because it takes skill—requiring study and practice—to be in a position to exploit the opportunities the casino presents. Nevertheless, a mere hour or two spent learning strategies for the beatable games will put you light-years ahead of the vast majority of visitors who give the gambling industry an average 12% to 15% profit margin.

THE GAMES

BACCARAT

The most "glamorous" game in the casino, baccarat is a version of *chemin de fer,* which is popular in European gambling halls. It's a favorite with high rollers because thousands of dollars are often staked on one hand. The Italian word *baccara* means "zero." This refers to the point value of 10s and picture cards. The game is run by four pit personnel. Two dealers sit side by side at the middle of the table. They handle the winning and losing bets and keep track of each player's "commission" *(explained below).* The caller stands in the middle of the other side of the table and dictates the action. The "ladderman" supervises the game and acts as final judge if any disputes arise.

HOW TO PLAY

Baccarat is played with eight decks of cards dealt from a large "shoe" (or cardholder). Each player is offered a turn at handling the shoe and dealing the cards. Two two-card hands are dealt facedown: the "player" and the "bank" hands. The player who deals the cards is called the banker, although the house banks both hands. The players bet on which hand—player or banker—will come closest to adding up to 9 (a "natural"). Ace through 9 retain face value, and 10s and picture cards are worth zero. If you have a hand adding up to more than 10, the number 10 is subtracted from the total. For example, if one hand contains a 10 and a 4, the hand adds up to 4. If the other holds an ace and a 6, it adds up to 7. If a hand has a 7 and a 9, it adds up to 6.

Depending on the two hands, the caller either declares a winner and loser (if either hand actually adds up to 8 or 9) or calls for another card for the player hand (if it totals 1, 2, 3, 4, 5, or 10). The bank hand then either stands pat or draws a card, determined by a complex series of rules depending on what the player's total is and dictated by the caller. When one or the other hand is declared a winner, the dealers go into action to pay off the winning wagers, collect the losing wagers, and add up the commission (usually 5%) that the house collects on the bank hand. Both bets have a house advantage of slightly more than 1%.

The player-dealer (or banker) holds the shoe as long as the bank hand wins. When the player hand wins, the shoe moves counterclockwise around the table. Players can refuse the shoe and pass it to the next player. Because the caller dictates the action, player responsibilities are minimal. It's not necessary to know the card-drawing rules, even if you're the banker.

BACCARAT STRATEGY

To bet, you only have to place your money in the bank, player, or tie box on the layout, which appears directly in front of where you sit. If you're betting that the bank hand will win, you put your chips in the bank box; bets for the player hand go in the player box. (Only real suckers bet on the tie.) Most players bet on the bank hand when they deal, since they "represent" the bank and to do otherwise would seem as if they were betting "against" themselves.

This isn't really true, but it seems that way. Playing baccarat is a simple matter of guessing whether the player or banker hand will come closest to 9 and deciding how much to bet on the outcome.

BLACKJACK

HOW TO PLAY

You play blackjack against a dealer, and whichever of you comes closest to a card total of 21 wins. Number cards are worth their face value, picture cards are worth 10, and aces are worth either 1 or 11. (Hands with aces are known as "soft" hands. Always count the ace first as an 11. If you also have a 10, your total will be 21, not 11.) If the dealer has a 17 and you have a 16, you lose. If you have an 18 against a dealer's 17, you win (even money). If both you and the dealer have a 17, it's a tie (or "push") and no money changes hands. If you go over a total of 21 (or "bust"), you lose, even if the dealer also busts later in the hand. If your first two cards add up to 21 (a "natural"), you're paid 3 to 2. But if the dealer also has a natural, it's a push. A natural beats a total of 21 achieved with more than two cards.

You're dealt two cards, either facedown or faceup, depending on the custom of the casino. The dealer also gives herself two cards, one facedown and one faceup (except in double-exposure blackjack, where both the dealer's cards are visible). Depending on your first two cards and the dealer's up card, you can **stand,** or refuse to take another card. You can **hit,** or take as many cards as you need until you stand or bust. You can **double down,** or double your bet and take one card. You can **split** a like pair; if you're dealt two 8s, for example, you can double your bet and play the 8s as if they're two hands. You can **buy insurance** if the dealer is showing an ace. Here you're wagering half your initial bet that the dealer *does* have a natural. If so, you lose your initial bet but are paid 2 to 1 on the insurance (which means the whole thing is a push). You can **surrender** half your initial bet if you're holding a bad hand (known as a "stiff") such as a 15 or 16 against a high-up card such as a 9 or 10.

BLACKJACK STRATEGY

Many people devote a great deal of time to learning complicated statistical schemes. But if you don't have the time, energy, or inclination to get that seriously involved, the following basic strategies should allow you to play the game with a modicum of skill and a paucity of humiliation:

When your hand is a total of 12, 13, 14, 15, or 16, and the dealer shows a 2, 3, 4, 5, or 6, you should stand. *Exception:* If your hand totals 12, and the dealer shows a 2 or 3, you should hit.

When your hand totals 12, 13, 14, 15, or 16, and the dealer shows a 7, 8, 9, 10, or ace, always hit.

When you hold 17, 18, 19, or 20, always stand.

When you hold a 10 or 11 and the dealer shows a 2, 3, 4, 5, 6, 7, 8, or 9, always double down.

When you hold a pair of aces or a pair of 8s, always split.

Never buy insurance.

CRAPS

Craps is a fast-paced, action-packed dice game that can require up to four pit personnel to run. Two dealers handle the bets made on either side of the layout. A "stickman" wields the long wooden stick, curved at one end, which is used to move the dice around the table. The stickman also calls the number that's rolled and books the proposition bets made in the middle of the layout. The "boxman" sits between the two dealers, overseeing the game and settling any disputes.

HOW TO PLAY

Stand at the table wherever you can find an open space. You can start betting casino chips immediately, but you have to wait your turn to be the shooter. The dice are passed clockwise around the table (the stickman will give you the dice at the appropriate time). It's important, when you're the shooter, to roll the dice hard enough so they bounce off the end wall of the table. This shows that you're not trying to control the dice with a "soft roll."

CRAPS STRATEGY

Playing craps is fairly straightforward; it's the betting that's complicated. The basic concepts are as follows: If the first time the shooter rolls the dice he or she turns up a 7 or 11, that's called a "natural"—an automatic win. If a 2, 3, or 12 comes up on the first throw (called the "come-out roll"), that's termed "craps"—an automatic lose. Each of the numbers 4, 5, 6, 8, 9, or 10 on a first roll is known as a "point": the shooter keeps rolling the dice until the point comes up again. If a 7 turns up before the point does, that's another loser.

When either the point or a losing 7 is rolled, this is known as a "decision," which happens on average every 3.3 rolls.

But "winning" and "losing" rolls of the dice are entirely relative in this game, because there are two ways you can bet at craps: "for" the shooter or "against" the shooter. Betting for means that the shooter will "make his point" (win). Betting against means that the shooter will "seven out" (lose). Either way, you're actually betting against the house, which books all wagers. If you're betting "for" on the come-out, you place your chips on the layout's "pass line." If a 7 or 11 is rolled, you win even money. If a 2, 3, or 12 (craps) is rolled, you lose your bet. If you're betting "against" on the come-out, you place your chips in the "don't pass bar." A 7 or 11 loses; a 2, 3, or 12 wins. A shooter can bet for or against himself, or against other players.

There are also roughly two dozen wagers you can make on any single specific roll of the dice. Craps strategy books can give you the details on come/don't come, odds, place, buy, big six, field, and proposition bets.

ROULETTE

Roulette is a casino game that uses a perfectly balanced wheel with 38 numbers (0, 00, and 1 through 36), a small white ball, a large layout with 11 different betting options, and special "wheel chips." The layout organizes 11 different bets into 6 "inside bets" (the single numbers, or those closest to the dealer) and 5 "outside bets" (the grouped bets, or those closest to the players).

The dealer spins the wheel clockwise and the ball counterclockwise. When the ball slows, the dealer announces, "No more bets." The ball drops from the "back track" to the "bottom track," caroming off built-in brass barriers and bouncing in and out of the different cups in the wheel before settling into the cup of the winning number. Then the dealer places a marker on the number and scoops all the losing chips into her corner. Depending on how crowded the game is, the casino can count on roughly 50 spins of the wheel per hour.

HOW TO PLAY

To buy in, place your cash on the layout near the wheel. Inform the dealer of the denomination of the individual unit you intend to play. Know the table limits (displayed on a sign in the dealer area). Don't ask for a 25¢ denomination if the minimum is $1. The dealer gives you a stack of wheel chips of a color that's different from those of all the other players and places a chip marker atop one of your wheel chips on the rim of the wheel to identify its denomination. Note that you must cash in your wheel chips at the roulette table before you leave the game. Only the dealer can verify how much they're worth.

ROULETTE STRATEGY

With **inside bets,** you can lay any number of chips (depending on the table limits) on a single number, 1 through 36 or 0 or 00. If the number hits, your payoff is 35 to 1, for a return of $36. You could, conceivably, place a $1 chip on all 38 numbers, but the return of $36 would leave you $2 short, which divides out to 5.26%, the house advantage. If you place a chip on the line between two numbers and one of those numbers hits, you're paid 17 to 1 for a return of $18 (again, $2 short of the true odds). Betting on three numbers returns 11 to 1, four numbers returns 8 to 1, five numbers pays 6 to 1 (this is the worst bet at roulette, with a 7.89% disadvantage), and six numbers pays 5 to 1.

To place an **outside bet,** lay a chip on one of three "columns" at the lower end of the layout next to numbers 34, 35, and 36. This pays 2 to 1. A bet placed in the first 12, second 12, or third 12 boxes also pays 2 to 1. A bet on red or black, odd or even, and 1 through 18 or 19 through 36 pays off at even money, 1 to 1. If you think you can bet on red *and* black, or odd *and* even, in order to play roulette and drink for free all night, think again. The green 0 or 00, which fall outside these two basic categories, will come up on average once every 19 spins of the wheel.

SLOT MACHINES

HOW TO PLAY

Playing slots is basically the same as it's always been. But the look and feel of the games has changed dramatically in the last several years. Machines that used to dispense a noisy waterfall of coins have all but given way to new generations of machines that pay out wins with printed coded tickets instead of coins. If you are a historian, or sentimental, you can still find a few coin-dispensing relics, but in the larger casinos they've almost all been replaced by the new ticketing payout system. These tickets can be inserted into other slot machines like cash, or can be redeemed at the cage or at ATM-like machines that dispense cash right on the casino floor. Nowadays many of the games are all-digital, with touch screens, and play like video games.

A roulette table at the Marriott's Stellaris Casino

But the underlying concept is still the same: after you start the game, you're looking for the reels—real or virtual—to match a winning pattern of shapes.

SLOT-MACHINE STRATEGY

The house advantage on slots varies from machine to machine, between 3% and 25%. Casinos that advertise a 97% payback are telling you that at least one of their slot machines has a house advantage of 3%. Which one? There's really no way of knowing. Generally, $1 machines pay back at a higher percentage than 25¢ or 5¢ machines. On the other hand, machines with smaller jackpots pay back more money more frequently, meaning that you'll be playing with more of your winnings.

One of the all-time great myths about slot machines is that they're "due" for a jackpot. Slots, like roulette, craps, keno, and Big Six, are subject to the Law of Independent Trials, which means the odds are permanently and unalterably fixed. If the odds of lining up three sevens on a 25¢ slot machine have been set by the casino at 1 in 10,000, then those odds remain 1 in 10,000 whether the three 7s have been hit three times in a row or not hit for 90,000 plays. Don't waste a lot of time playing a machine that you suspect is "ready," and don't think if someone hits a jackpot on a particular machine only minutes after you've finished playing on it that it was "yours."

VIDEO POKER
This section deals only with straight-draw video poker.

Like blackjack, video poker is a game of strategy and skill, and at select times on select machines the player actually holds the advantage, however slight, over the house. Unlike with slot machines, you can determine the exact edge of video-poker machines. Like slots, however, video-poker machines are often tied into a progressive meter; when the jackpot total reaches high enough, you can beat the casino at its own game. The variety of video-poker machines is growing steadily. All are played in similar fashion, but the strategies are different.

HOW TO PLAY
The schedule for the payback on winning hands is posted on the machine, usually above the screen. It lists the returns for a high pair (generally jacks or better), two pair, three of a kind, a flush, full house, straight flush, four of a kind, and royal flush, depending on the number of coins played— usually 1, 2, 3, 4, or 5. Look for machines that pay with a single coin played: one coin for "jacks or better" (meaning a pair of jacks, queens, kings, or aces; any other pair is a stiff), two coins for two pairs, three for three of a kind, six for a flush, nine for a full house, 50 for a straight flush, 100 for four of a kind, and 250 for a royal flush. This is known as a 9/6 machine—one that gives a nine-coin payback for a full house and a six-coin payback for a flush with one coin played. Other machines are known as 8/5 (eight for a full house, five for a flush), 7/5, and 6/5.

You want a 9/6 machine because it gives you the best odds: the return from a standard 9/6 straight-draw machine is 99.5%; you give up only half a percent to the house. An 8/5 machine returns 97.3%. On 6/5 machines, the figure drops to 95.1%, slightly less than roulette. Machines with varying paybacks are scattered throughout the casinos. In some you'll see an 8/5 machine right next to a 9/6, and someone will be blithely playing the 8/5 machine.

As with slot machines, it's optimum to play the maximum number of coins to qualify for the jackpot. You insert five coins into the slot and press the "deal" button. Five cards appear on the screen—say, 5, jack, queen, 5, 9. To hold the pair of 5s, you press the hold buttons under the first and fourth cards. The word "hold" appears underneath the two 5s. You then press the "draw" button (often the same button as "deal") and three new cards appear on the screen—say, 10, jack, 5. You have three 5s. With five coins bet, the machine will give you 15 credits. Now you can press the "max bet" button: five units will be removed from your credits, and five new cards will appear on the screen. You repeat the hold-and-draw process; if you hit a winning hand, the proper payback will be added to your credits.

VIDEO-POKER STRATEGY

Like blackjack, video poker has a basic strategy that's been formulated by the computer simulation of hundreds of millions of hands. The most effective way to learn it is with a video poker–computer program that deals the cards on your screen, then tutors you in how to play each hand properly. If you don't want to devote that much time to the study of video poker, memorizing these six rules will help you make the right decision for more than half the hands you'll be dealt:

If you're dealt a completely "stiff" hand (no like cards and no picture cards), draw five new cards.

If you're dealt a hand with no like cards but with one jack, queen, king, or ace, always hold on to the picture card; if you're dealt two different picture cards, hold both. But if you're dealt three different picture cards, hold only two (the two of the same suit, if that's an option).

If you're dealt a pair, hold it, no matter the face value.

Never hold a picture card with a pair of 2s through 10s.

Never draw two cards to try for a straight or a flush.

Never draw one card to try for an inside straight.

RECOMMENDED CASINOS

Most casinos are found in hotels; all are along Palm Beach or Eagle Beach or in downtown Oranjestad. Although the minimum age to enter is 18, some venues are relaxed about this rule. By day "barefoot elegance" is the norm in all casinos, although many establishments have a shirt-and-shoes requirement. Evening dress is expected to be more polished, though still casual. In high season the casinos are open from just before noon to the wee hours; in low season (May to November) they may not start dealing until late afternoon.

If you plan to play large sums of money, check in with the casino upon arrival so that you can be rewarded for your business. Some hotels offer gambling goodies—complimentary meals at local restaurants, chauffeured tours, and, in the cases of big spenders, high-roller suites. Even small-scale gamblers may be entitled to coupons for meals and discounted rooms.

ORANJESTAD AND ENVIRONS

Crystal Casino. Adorned with Austrian crystal chandeliers and gold-leaf columns, the Renaissance Aruba's glittering casino evokes Monaco's grand establishments. The Salon Privé offers serious gamblers a private room for baccarat, roulette, and high-stakes blackjack. This casino is popular among cruise-ship passengers, who stroll over from the port to watch and play in slot tournaments and bet on sporting events. Luxury car giveaways are also a big draw there. It's open 24 hours. ⊠ *Renaissance Aruba Resort & Casino, L.G. Smith Blvd. 82, Oranjestad* ☏ *297/583–6000 ext. 6318.*

★ Fodor'sChoice **Seaport Casino.** A super-lively and fun casino right on the waterfront and across the street from the lively Renaissance Marketplace, this place has more than 300 modern slots as well as six blackjack tables, Caribbean stud, roulette, regular poker, and Texas hold 'em. Sister to Crystal Casino close by, they give away luxury cars and offer free play slot cards. They also have state-of-the-art race and sports book operations. It's open until 6 am. ⊠ *L. G. Smith Blvd. 9, Oranjestad* ☏ *297/583–6000 ext. 6318.*

DRUIF

★ Fodor'sChoice **Alhambra Casino.** Part of the Divi family and accessible by golf cart from the company's all-inclusive resorts, this is a lively popular casino with a big selection of modern slots, blackjack, craps, poker, roulette, and more. Be sure to join their Player's Club—it's free and offers free slot credits, and you earn points with your card as well. The Cove restaurant serves light meals and drinks; you'll also receive free drinks on the floor when you're playing the games. Special theme nights and promotions run all week, and on Saturday afternoons the casino hosts Super Bingo. ⊠ *L.G. Smith Blvd. 47, Druif* ☏ *297/583–5000* ⊕ *www. casinoalhambra.com.*

EAGLE BEACH

Glitz Casino. A colorful, friendly little enclave, the casino oftens hosts live bands who play overlooking a big sunken bar called The Liquid Lounge. The usual assortment of games includes poker, blackjack, and over 200 slots. There are fun promotions and raffles almost daily, too. ⊠ *La Cabana Resort, J.E. Irausquin Blvd. 250, Eagle Beach* ☎ *297/587–3399* ⊕ *www.glitz-casino.com.*

PALM BEACH AND NOORD

★ Fodor'sChoice **The Casino at the Ritz-Carlton.** A very "ritzy" casino just off the lobby of the Ritz-Carlton Aruba offers many traditional table games like blackjack, craps, roulette, Caribbean Stud poker, baccarat, and Texas hold 'em and more than 300 snazzy modern slots: spinning reels, video reels, and video games with jackpots available 24/7. Tables run from 6 pm to 3 am. They also have two sports-betting kiosks and offer "luxury" bingo several times a week. Points accumulated from their VIP casino club card can be used toward hotel extras like dining, spa treatments, and room nights. ⊠ *L. G. Smith Blvd. 107, Palm Beach* ☎ *297/527–2222* ⊕ *www.ritzcarlton.com.*

The Casino at the Hilton. Famous for its starry indoor skies, this casino is smaller than some, but it remains very popular with locals as well as visitors. Somewhat refreshed since the Hilton took over the Radisson, it is still basically the same spot with typical slots, gaming tables, and good poker action. Nice additions are the extra events like Ladies' Night Bingo and free-play fever raffles. The loyalty program allows players to gain points for Hilton resort extras as well as casino bonuses. It's open until 3 am. ⊠ *J. E. Irausquin Blvd. 81, Palm Beach* ☎ *297/526–6930* ⊕ *www3.hilton.com.*

Excelsior Casino. Located in the Holiday Inn Aruba Resort, this is one of the oldest casinos on the island, and unfortunately its age is beginning to show. Many sections in the common areas are somewhat rundown and the air-filtering system could use an upgrade, but there is still a good selection of standard slots, blackjack, craps, and roulette tables, and the place is usually hopping with locals for daily bingo games. The blackjack tables are known for not hitting "the soft 17." ⊠ *Holiday Inn Resort Aruba, J. E. Irausquin Blvd. 230, Palm Beach* ☎ *297/586–7777, 297/586–3600* ⊕ *www. excelsiorcasino.com.*

Good-Luck Charms

Arubans take myths and superstitions very seriously. They flinch if a black butterfly flits into their home, because this symbolizes death. And on New Year's Eve they toss the first sips of whiskey, rum, or champagne from the first bottle that's opened in the New Year out the door of their house to show respect to those who have died and to wish luck on others. It's no surprise, then, that good-luck charms are part of Aruba's casino culture as well.

The island's most common good-luck charm is the *djucu* (pronounced *joo*-koo), a brown-and-black stone that comes from the sea and becomes hot when rubbed. It's often called the "lucky nut." Many people have them put in gold settings—with their initials engraved in the metal—and wear them around their necks on a chain with other charms such as an anchor or a cross. Another item that's thought to bring good luck is a small bag of sand. The older generation of women might wear them tucked discreetly into their bras.

Hyatt Regency Casino. Ablaze with neon, with a Carnival-in-Rio theme the Copacabana casino at the Hyatt is always buzzing with action. The most popular games are slots, blackjack, craps, and baccarat, but you will also find over 200 modern slots. This gambling emporium is also known for its live music Thursday through Sunday and lively party atmosphere. Don't forget to ask for your $10 free play card (ID required). It's open until 4 am. ⊠ *Hyatt Regency Aruba Beach Resort & Casino, J.E. Irausquin Blvd. 85, Palm Beach* ☎ *297/586–1234* ⊕ *www.aruba.hyatt.com.*

Liv Casino. A small but welcoming little casino is just off the lobby of Barcelo Aruba Resort. It's a great spot to try your luck at some brand-new slot games. There are also some interesting promotions, including "Senior Days." ⊠ *Barcelo Aruba Resort.Palm Beach, J.E. Irausquin Blvd. 82, Palm Beach* ☎ *297/586–4500.*

Orchid Casino. This lively casino is also popular with locals for blackjack, roulette, craps, Caribbean poker, and baccarat; those are in addition to some 300 slot machines. The vibe is fresh and modern. With 12 gaming tables and more live poker games than anywhere else on the island, it's your best bet if you are looking for the weekly poker tournament. A Sports and Race Book is also on-site. It's

7

open until 4 am. ✉ *RIU Palace Antillas, J.E. Irausquin Blvd. 77, Palm Beach* ☎ *297/525–7777* ⊕ *www.westinaruba.com.*

★ Fodor'sChoice **Stellaris Casino.** This is the largest casino on the island and offers 500 modern interactive slots as well as 28 tables with games like craps, roulette, poker, and blackjack. There's a state-of-the-art race and sports betting operation. Don't forget to join the VIP Club program, where you can earn points, comps, and prizes. They offer free cocktails for gamers, and there are many special theme and entertainment nights. ✉ *Aruba Marriott Resort, L.G. Smith Blvd. 101, Palm Beach* ☎ *297/586–9000* ⊕ *www. stellariscasino.com.*

SPORTS AND THE OUTDOORS

ON ARUBA YOU CAN HIKE a surreal arid outback and participate in every conceivable water sport, play tennis or golf, and horseback ride along the sea. But the big sport of note these days is beach tennis. Aruba has become the beach tennis capital of the Caribbean, and Palm and Eagle Beaches host several tournaments, including one big annual international competition. As for water sports, the coolest new thing to do on Aruba is the thrilling jet-pack-over-water ride called Jetlev. They also offer hoverboard—an air-propelled skateboard over the waves—and jet blades, which are like ski boots on a board that jet-blast you into the air. Parasailing, banana boats, kayaking, paddleboarding, even yoga on paddleboard .. You name it, Aruba has it. And this island has some of the world's best conditions for windsurfing and kiteboarding. In fact, it has produced world champions.

BIKING AND MOTORCYCLING

Cycling is a great way to get around the island—though biking along busy roads is not encouraged—the new Linear Park paved trail from downtown Oranjestad all the way to the airport is ideal for families seeking a biking adventure along the sea. New Green Bike kiosks dotted all over the island (there are eight stations now, with more to come) make it easy to grab a bike and deposit it at another station when you're done. If you'd rather cycle with less exertion, there are electric-bike rentals at La Cabana Resort. Many resorts offer their guests coaster bikes for free (or for a low fee) to pedal around the beach areas, and there are also guided mountain bike tours that take you to the rugged interior. Or let your hair down completely and cruise around on a Harley-Davidson, either solo or with a group tour.

RENTALS

There are plenty of dealers who will be happy to help you in your motoring pursuits.

★ Fodor's Choice **Green Bike Aruba.** It's no surprise that this operation—the first bike-sharing program in the Caribbean—has become popular very quickly. But is it any wonder since Aruba is a Dutch-influenced island and people from the Netherlands adore their bikes? With over 100 modern bikes at eight stations dotted over the island (at busy tourist junctions including the cruise terminal), it's easy to swipe your credit card and hit the road. When you're done, park it somewhere

Relatively flat, Aruba is the perfect biking destination.

else for the next person. Rentals are by the hour or week. ☎ *297/594–6368* ⊕ *www.greenbikearuba.com* ✉ *From $12.*

George's Cycle Co. This outfit has been renting motorcycles, scooters, and ATVs since the late 1980s. It's a reputable firm that offers great vehicles at good prices. Hotel pickup and drop-off is available. ✉ *L.G. Smith Blvd. 124, Oranjestad* ☎ *297/593–2202* ⊕ *www.georgecycles.com* ✉ *From $55 per day.*

ORGANIZED EXCURSIONS

FAMILY **Aruba Active Vacations Mountain Biking Tours.** Unless you are a skilled cyclist, you are best to join a tour to explore the island's arid, rugged, and unforgiving outback. This outfitter offers 2½-hour guided tours on top-quality Cannondale bikes with water and helmets supplied, including pickup and drop-off at your hotel. Points of interest include Alto Vista Chapel and the California Lighthouse, and the tour begins at the company's windsurfing shop at Fisherman's Huts. ✉ *Fisherman's Huts Beach, Malmokweg* ☎ *297/586–0989* ⊕ *www.aruba-active-vacations.com* ✉ *From $55.*

★ Fodor'sChoice **Aruba E-Bike Tours.** Only one island operator offers fat-tire electric bicycles that can give you a power boost when you need it. Visitors can choose any one of four hour-long guided tours around the island. There are daily departures in the early morning and at sunset, and points

8

of interest include the California Lighthouse and Alto Vista Chapel. Helmets and visibilty vests are included. Children must be 12 and over. ⊠ *Paseo Herencia Mall, J.E. Irausquin Blvd. 328A, Palm Beach* ☎ *297/592–5550* ⊕ *www.arubae-biketours.com* 🖃 *From $45.*

Aruba Motorcycle Tours. Hog fans will adore this novel way to tour Aruba. On your own Harley with a rental, or in one of their guided group tours—a four-hour trip that takes only the back roads to bring you the island's best sites—you will enjoy the open road like a rebel with this outfit. A motorcycle license and $1,000 deposit is required with each tour. For rentals alone, a $2,000 deposit is required. Helmets are supplied, and pickup and drop-off at hotels is offered. All renters and group riders must be over 21. ⊠ *Jaburibari 16-C, Paradera* ☎ *297/ 641–7818* ⊕ *www.arubamotorcycletours.com* 🖃 *Tours from $20 (on top of rental).*

★ Fodor'sChoice **Green Bike Aruba Tours.** The same company that supplies the grab-and-go shared bike kiosks around the island also offers two group bike tours. One explores the beaches around the California Lighthouse and includes a stop there, and the other explores downtown and the Linear Park. Both tours include a well-informed guide, a bike cooler basket with snacks and water, and free Wi-Fi as you tour. Bring or wear your bathing suit as they take swim stops, too. ⊠ *Caya Ernesto Petronia 69, Oranjestad* ☎ *297/593–6368* ⊕ *www.greenbikearuba.com* 🖃 *From $39.*

BOWLING

★ Fodor'sChoice **Dream Bowl Aruba.** Dream Bowl does it right
FAMILY with eight glow-in-the-dark bowling lanes, hip music, computerized scoring, and all kinds of special theme nights with prizes. It's part of the larger entertainment emporium on the top floors of the modern Palm Beach Plaza that includes a huge video arcade, a big modern sports bar, billiard tables, a food court, and prize machines. There is also a karaoke room and photo booth. ⊠ *Palm Beach Plaza, L. G. Smith Blvd. 95, Suite 310, Palm Beach* ☎ *297/586–0809* 🖃 *From $35.*

FAMILY **Eagle Bowling Palace.** Arubans love to bowl and often compete off-island. The Eagle emporium is the local favorite spot. Close to the high-rise strip, it has computerized lanes, a snack bar, and a cocktail lounge. Equipment rentals and group rates are available. ⊠ *Sasakiweg, Pos Abao* ☎ *297/583–5038* 🖃 *From $35.*

DAY SAILS

Aruba is not much of a sailing destination, though you will see a lot of luxury catamarans taking big groups of tourists out for a fun day of party sailing, snorkeling tours, or sunset dinner cruises. The main operators for large groups are DePalm, Red Sail, and Pelican. All have large catamarans, but some companies also offer old-fashioned wooden schooners for their day sails and snorkeling trips. There are a few smaller private yacht charters available as well. The weather is typically ideal, the waters are calm and clear, and the trade winds are gentle, so there's never really a bad time to hit the waves.

Many of these day sails include stops for snorkeling, but the companies recommended here offer more than just a snorkel tour, often including drinks and loud music.

Day sails usually take off from either DePalm Pier, Hadicurari Pier, or Pelican Pier on Palm Beach. Many tour companies include pickup and drop-off service at the major resorts.

★ Fodor's Choice **Jolly Pirates.** Aruba's unique, pirate-themed sailing adventure is a rollicking ride aboard a big, beautiful teak schooner replete with a wild and crazy swashbuckling crew and an open bar. The boat offers snorkeling tours with two or three stops and a rope swing adventure, and the sunset cruises are also first-rate. Prepare to party hearty as it's bascially impossible not to due to their signature "pirate's poisen" rum punch and infectious loud music. Snorkel trips always include the *Antilla* wreck. Departures are from Hadicurari Pier behind MooMba Beach Bar. ⊠ *Hadicurari Pier, Palm Beach* ✚ *Behind MooMba Beach Bar* ☎ 586–8107 ⊕ *www.jolly-pirates.com* 🖂 *From $42.*

FAMILY **Mi Dushi.** *Mi Dushi* means "my sweetheart" in the local lingo, and this operator has been offering guests snorkeling and sailing trips on Aruban waters for more than three decades. The company's vessel is a huge, colorful four-deck catamaran than can hold up to 70 people. Tours include music, an open bar, snorkel gear, instruction, and a pirate rope swing. Snorkel tours cover Aruba's three most popular reefs, and romantic sunset sails are also available. You can also charter them for private parties. Excursions depart from the Hadicurari Pier on Palm Beach. ⊠ *Hadicurari Pier, Palm Beach* ✚ *Next to Marriott's Surf Club* ☎ 297/640–3000 ⊕ *www.midushi.com* 🖂 *From $40.*

Snorkeling from a replica pirate ship

Montforte III. Take your sailing experience up a notch aboard this luxurious teak schooner that is designed to pamper. Exclusive tours take you to spots like Spanish Lagoon for snorkeling and kayaking, and around Boca Catalina for four-course dinners under the stars. Unlimited premium spirits, signature cocktails, tapas, and snacks are included in all trips, and there's sometimes live music on board as well. Departure is from Pelican Pier. ⊠ *Pelican Pier, Palm Beach* ☎ *297/583–0400* ⊕ *www.montfortcruise.com* ⊠ *From $125.*

★ **Fodor'sChoice Sailaway Tours Aruba.** Hop aboard the *Lady Black,* the newest vessel to hit Aruba's high seas. At 110 feet, this beautifully retrofitted old-fashioned wooden schooner is now also the largest party ship on the island. Enjoy an open bar and a big rope hammock on the bow while you sail with one of their snorkel, sunset, or dinner cruises. The friendly crew are happy to help you try some antics on the rope swing, and you can even hop on board their backs while they do flips into the water. The party can get crazy. Available for private charters as well. ⊠ *Hadicurari Pier, Palm Beach* ⊹ *Look for their sign to check-in across from MooMba Beach Bar in front of Hadicurari Pier* ☎ *297/739–9000* ⊕ *www.sailawaytour.com* ⊠ *From $47.*

Tranquilo Charters Aruba. Captain Mike Hagedoorn, a legendary Aruban sailor, handed the helm over to his son Captain Anthony a few years ago after 20 years of running the family business. Today, *The Tranquilo*—a 43-foot sailing yacht—still takes small groups of passengers to a secluded spot at a Spanish lagoon named Mike's Reef, where not many other snorkel trips venture. The lunch cruise to the south side always includes "Mom's famous Dutch pea soup," and they also do private charters for dinner sails and sailing trips around Aruba's lesser-explored coasts. Look for the red boat docked at the Renaissance Marina beside the Atlantis Submarine launch. ⊠ *Renaissance Marina, Oranjestad* ☎ *297/586–1418* ⊕ *www.tranquiloaruba.com* ⊠ *From $85.*

FISHING

Deep-sea catches here include anything from barracuda, tuna, and wahoo to kingfish, sailfish, and marlins. A few skippered charter boats are available for half- or full-day excursions. Package prices vary but typically include tackle, bait, and refreshments.

★ Fodor'sChoice **Driftwood Charters.** *Driftwood1* is a tournament-rigged, 35-foot yacht manned by Captain Herby, who is famous for offering deep-sea fishing charters on Aruba since the early 1990s. He is also co-owner of Driftwood Restaurant and is always happy to bring your catch to their chef for expert preparation so you can enjoy it for dinner the very same night. Charters can accommodate up to six people. ⊠ *Seaport Marina, Oranjestad* ☎ *297/583–2515* ⊕ *driftwoodfishingcharters.com* ⊠ *From $400.*

FAMILY **Teaser Fishing Charters Aruba.** The expertise of the Teaser crew is matched by a commitment to sensible fishing practices, which include catch and release and avoiding ecologically sensitive areas. The company's yacht is fully equipped, and the crew seem to have an uncanny ability to locate the best fishing spots with Captain Milton at the helm. ⊠ *Renaissance Marina, Oranjestad* ☎ *297/593–9228* ⊕ *teaserfishingaruba.com* ⊠ *From $400.*

GOLF

Golf may seem incongruous on an arid island such as Aruba, yet there are several popular courses. Trade winds and the occasional stray goat add unexpected hazards.

The Links at Divi Aruba. This 9-hole course was designed by Karl Litten and Lorie Viola. The par-36 flat layout stretches to 2,952 yards and features paspalum grass (best for seaside courses) and takes you past beautiful lagoons. It's a testy little course with water abounding, making accuracy more important than distance. Amenities include a golf school with professional instruction, a driving range, a practice green, and a two-story golf clubhouse with a pro shop. Two restaurants are available: Windows on Aruba for fine dining and Mulligan's for a casual and quick lunch. ⊠ *Divi Village Golf & Beach Resort, J.E. Irausquin Blvd. 93, Druif* ☎ *297/581–4653* ⊕ *www.divilinks.com* ☎ *From $90* ⚲ *9 holes, 2952 yards, par 36.*

★ Fodor'sChoice **Tierra del Sol.** Stretching out to 6,811 yards, this stunning course is situated on the northwest coast near the California Lighthouse and is Aruba's only 18-hole course. It hosted its first PGA-sanctioned event, the Aruba Cup, in 2016. Designed by Robert Trent Jones Jr., Tierra del Sol combines Aruba's native beauty—cacti and rock formations, stunning views—with good greens and beautiful landscaping. Wind can also be a factor here on the rolling terrain, as are the abundant bunkers and water hazards. Greens fees include a golf cart equipped with GPS and a communications system that allows you to order drinks for your return to the clubhouse. The fully stocked golf shop is one of the Caribbean's most elegant, with an extremely attentive staff. ⊠ *Tierra del Sol Resort, Caya di Solo 10, Malmokweg* ☎ *297/586–7800* ⊕ *www.tierradelsol.com/golf/* ☎ *From $129* ⚲ *18 holes, 6811 yards, par 71.*

HIKING

Despite Aruba's arid landscape, hiking the rugged countryside will give you the best opportunities to see the island's wildlife and flora. Arikok National Park is an excellent place to glimpse the real Aruba, free of the trappings of tourism. The heat can be oppressive, so be sure to take it easy, wear a hat, and have a bottle of water handy. Get maps and information at Arikok National Park Visitor Center.

★ Fodor'sChoice **Arikok National Park.** There are more than 20

FAMILY miles (34 km) of trails concentrated in the island's eastern interior and along its northeastern coast. Arikok Park is crowned by Aruba's second-highest mountain, the 577-foot Mt. Arikok, so you can also go climbing there.

Hiking in the park, whether alone or in a group led by guides, is generally not too strenuous. You'll need sturdy shoes to grip the granular surfaces and climb the occasion-

CLOSE UP

'"Go On with the Struggle"

Arubans are proud of their autonomous standing within the Kingdom of the Netherlands, and Gilberto François "Betico" Croes is heralded as the hero behind the island's *status aparte* (separate status). His birthday, January 25, is an official Aruban holiday.

During the Dutch colonial expansion of the 17th century, Aruba and five other islands—Bonaire, Curaçao, St. Maarten, St. Eustatius, and Saba—became territories known as the Netherlands Antilles. After World War II these islands began to pressure Holland for autonomy, and in 1954 they became a collective self-governing entity under the umbrella of the Kingdom of the Netherlands.

At that time, several political parties were in power on the island. Soon, however, Juancho Irausquin (who has a major thoroughfare named in his honor) formed a new party that maintained control for

nearly two decades. Irausquin was considered the founder of Aruba's new economic order and the precursor of modern Aruban politics. After his death his party's power diminished.

In 1971 Croes, then a young, ambitious school administrator, became the leader of another political party. Bolstered by a thriving economy generated by Aruba's oil refinery, Croes spearheaded the island's cause to secede from the Netherlands Antilles and to gain status as an equal partner within the Dutch kingdom. Sadly, he didn't live to celebrate the realization of his dream. On December 31, 1985, the day before Aruba's new status became official, Croes was in a car accident that put him in a coma for 11 months. He died on November 26, 1986. Etched in the minds of Arubans are his prophetic words: *Si mi cai na cominda, gara e bandera y sigui cu e lucha* ("If I die along the way, seize the flag and go on with the struggle").

8

ally steep terrain. You should also exercise caution with the strong sun—bring along plenty of water and wear sunscreen and a hat. At the park's main entrance, the Arikok Visitor Center houses exhibits, restrooms, and food facilities and provides maps and marked trail information, park rules, and features. Free guided mini-tours are the best way to get oriented at the park entrance. You can also download hiking maps from their online website for self-guided tours. ⊠ *Santa Cruz* ☎ *297/585–1234* ⊕ *www.arubanationalpark. org* 🎫 *$11 (park entrance)* ⊙ *Park closes at 4 pm.*

FAMILY **Nature Sensitive Tours.** Eddy Croes, a former park ranger whose passion for nature is infectious, runs this outfitter with care. Groups are never larger than eight people, so you'll see as much detail as you can handle. The hikes are done at an easy pace and are suitable for just about anyone. Moonlight tours also available. If you'd rather not hike, Eddy also has a 4x4 monster jeep–guided tour of the arid outback for up to 20 people as well. ✉ *Pos Chiquito 13E, Savaneta* ☎ *297/585–1594* ⊕ *www.naturesensitivetours. com* ✇ *From $79.*

HORSEBACK RIDING

Ranches offer short jaunts along the beach or longer rides through the countryside and even to the ruins of an old gold mill. Riders of all experience levels will be thrilled that most of Aruba's horses are descendants of the Spanish Paso Fino—meaning "fine step"—which offer a supersmooth ride even at a trot!

★ Fodor's Choice **Rancho Daimari.** This operation offers some of
FAMILY the best horseback ridings tours on Aruba. Choose from a trek to the incredible natural pool in the heart of Arikok National Park, or to a scenic and secret surfer's beach. Tours are very family-friendly and accommodate all levels of riding skills. Complimentary return transportation from hotels. Reservations mandatory. ✉ *Daimari* ☎ *297/588– 8710* ⊕ *www.arubaranchodaimari.net* ✇ *From $105.*

★ Fodor's Choice **Rancho La Ponderosa.** Run by one of Aruba's
FAMILY best-known horsemen—and using steeds from his private stock—Rancho La Ponderosa offers quality rides of two or two-and-a-half hours. Choose from a route along the wild coast to gold mill ruins and a fallen land bridge, or ride the famous ostrich farm. It's noteworthy that these tours never encounter vehicular traffic. ✉ *Papaya 30, Paradera* ☎ *297/587– 1142* ⊕ *www.rancholaponderosa.com* ✇ *From $80.*

FAMILY **Rancho Notorious.** One of Aruba's oldest tour operators, Rancho Notorious offers horseback riding for all levels in the island's arid outback and beside scenic, rocky seasides where cars cannot venture. If you don't want to ride horses, you can also take one of many other guided tours, including ATV outback adventures and mountain biking trips. ✉ *Boroncana, Noord* ☎ *297/586–0508* ⊕ *www.ranchonotorious.com* ✇ *From $65.*

CLOSE UP

Sidney Ponson: Pitcher

When he was growing up in Aruba, Sidney Ponson loved sailing, scuba diving, and just about anything to do with the ocean. "My life was the beach," says Ponson, "before baseball." He started playing baseball when he was nine, even though the game was pretty difficult on an arid island where the fields are full of rocks. But employment on his uncle's boat taught him to work hard for what he wanted in life.

The pitcher signed with the minor leagues at 16, then was tapped by the Baltimore Orioles at 21. Hitting the big leagues involved lots of hard work (his grueling workouts last from 7:30 am to 1 pm and involve lifting weights, running, and throwing), but Ponson says it was worth it when he got the call to play. "It was 6:30 am, and I was on a road trip in a hotel in Scranton," he remembers. "They told me when to show up and said to be ready to play at 8:30."

Now Ponson is a free agent and spends much of his time in Aruba resting and visiting family and friends. Ponson used his status as a major leaguer to do some good for his island. He and fellow Aruban baseball player Calvin Maduro draft other professional baseball players, including Pedro Martinez and Manny Ramirez, to play in an annual celebrity softball game to raise funds for Aruba's Cas pa Hubentud, a home for underprivileged children.

He was awarded with the Order of Orange-Nassau by Queen Beatrix of the Netherlands in 2003.

Today Aruba has a new baseball star getting a lot of attention. Xander Jan Bogaerts plays as a shortstop/third baseman for the Boston Red Sox. He had the entire island on its feet when they won the World Series in 2013. He and his mother started a charitable foundation to help the island's local kids have easier access to organized sports and professional equipment. In 2016, the baseball park in his hometown of San Nicolas was renamed after him.

8

KAYAKING

Kayaking is a popular sport on Aruba, especially because the waters are so calm. It's a great way to explore the coast and the mangroves.

★ Fodor'sChoice **Aruba Outdoor Adventures.** This small, family-run
FAMILY outfitter offers a unique combination of small-group (six people max.) pedal-kayaking and snorkel tours along the island's southeastern coast. Mangroves and reef explo-

Kayaking in a sheltered cove

rations take you around calm water near Mangel Halto, Savaneta, and Barcadera; well-informed guides explain the natural environment and help guests navigate the snorkeling portions. No kayaking experience is neccessary. Pickup and drop-off are included, as well as snorkel equipment, a dry bag, snacks, and drinks. Departures are from the DePalm Island Ferry Terminal outside Oranjestad. ⊠ *Depalm Island Ferry Terminal, Balashi* ☎ *297/749–6646* ⊕ *www.arubaoutdooradventures.com* 🖃 *From $110.*

★ **Fodor's Choice Clear Kayak Aruba.** This is the only Aruba outfitter that offers clear-bottomed sea kayaks, and it's the only operator offering night sea tours as well. By day, groups paddle through the natural mangroves at Mangel Halto with a guide who can tell you how the roots create a natural nursery for juvenile marine life; the route also passes over lots of big healthy coral full of colorful tropical fish. A second tour begins at Arashi Beach at dusk, then after dark the kayaks are lit up with LED lights that will attract marine life to clear bottoms. You must be 12 or older to participate. ⊠ *Savaneta 402, Savaneta* ☎ *297/566–2205* ⊕ *www.clearkayakaruba.com* 🖃 *From $50.*

Wildlife Watching

Wildlife abounds on Aruba. Look for the cottontail rabbit: the black patch on its neck likens it to a species found in Venezuela, spawning a theory that it was brought to the island by pre-Columbian peoples. Wild donkeys, originally transported to the island by the Spanish, are found in the more rugged terrain; sheep and goats roam freely throughout the island.

About 170 bird species make their home on Aruba year-round, and migratory birds temporarily raise the total to 300 species when they fly by in November and January. Among the highlights are the *trupiaal* (bright orange), the *prikichi* (a parakeet with a green body and yellow head), and the *barika geel* (a small, yellow-bellied bird with a sweet tooth—you may find one eating the sugar off your breakfast table). At Bubali Bird Sanctuary, on the island's western side, you can see various types of waterfowl, especially cormorants, herons, scarlet ibis, and fish eagles. Along the south shore brown pelicans are common. At Tierra del Sol golf course in the north you may glimpse the *shoco*, the endangered burrowing owl. Lizard varieties include large

iguanas, once hunted for use in local soups and stews. (That practice is now illegal.) Like chameleons, these iguanas change color to adapt to their surroundings—from bright green when foraging in the foliage (which they love to eat) to a brownish shade when sunning themselves in the dirt. The *pega pega*—a cousin of the gecko—is named for the suction pads on its feet that allow it to grip virtually any surface (*pega* means "to stick" in Papiamento). The *kododo blauw* (whiptail lizard) is one of the species that's unique to the island.

Until a few years ago, only two types of snakes were found on Aruba: the cat-eyed *santanero*, which isn't venomous, and the poisonous *cascabel*, a unique subspecies of rattlesnake that doesn't use its rattle. But because of human error, the boa has also ended up on Aruba and is actively hunted because it is an invasive species that has no natural predators on the island. Its growing numbers have been wreaking havoc on the island's native species like the small burrowing owl—the shoco—recently named Aruba's national animal symbol.

MULTISPORT OUTFITTERS

There are a number of outfitters in Aruba that can handle nearly all your water- or land-based activities with guided excursions and rental equipment. Here is a list of a few of our favorites.

★ Fodor'sChoice **De Palm Tours.** Aruba's premier tour company
FAMILY covers every inch of the island on land and under sea, and they even have their own submarine (*Atlantis*) and semi-submarine (*Seaworld Explorer*) and their own all-inclusive private island destination (De Palm Island), which has both great diving and snorkeling as well as SNUBA and other activities. Land exploration options include air-conditioned bus sightseeing tours and rough and rugged outback jaunts by jeep safari to popular attractions like the natural pool. You can also do off-road tours in a UTV (two-seater utility task vehicle) via their guided caravan trips. On the waves, their luxury catamaran DePalm Pleasure offers romantic sunset sails and snorkel trips that include an option to try Snuba—deeper snorkeling with an air-supplied raft at Aruba's most famous shipwreck. DePalm also offers airport transfers. ✉ *L.G. Smith Blvd. 142, Oranjestad* ☎ *297/582–4400* ⊕ *www.depalmtours.com* ✇ *From $44.*

FAMILY **Pelican Adventures.** In operation since 1984, this company arranges sailing and boating charters for fishing and exploring, as well as jeep adventures and guided excursions to Aruba's caves and historic sites. Scuba and snorkeling trips are available for divers of all levels. Novices start with midmorning classes and then move to the pool to practice what they've learned; by afternoon they put their new skills to use at a shipwreck off the coast. The company is also known for its fun Havana-style sunset cruises and also a dinner cruise that chases the sunset then ends with a meal at the company's pier restaurant, Pelican Nest Seafood Grill. ✉ *Pelican Pier, Palm Beach ⊹ Near the Holiday Inn and Playa Linda hotels* ☎ *297/586–3271* ⊕ *www.pelican-aruba.com* ✇ *From $50.*

★ Fodor'sChoice **Red Sail Sports Aruba.** A dynamic company established in 1989, they are experts in the field of water-sports recreation. They offer excellent diving excursions, snorkel sails, sunset sails, and full dinner sails. The company also has its own sports equipment shops, and are the original operators to introduce the cool new sport of Jetlev—a personal jet pack over the water—and jet blades—like roller blades on the waves and hoverboards. Theirs are

the island's only certified instructors for these activities.
✉ *J.E. Irausquin Blvd. 348-A, Palm Beach* ☎ *297/586–1603*
⊕ *www.redsailaruba.com* ✉ *From $55.*

SCUBA DIVING AND SNORKELING

With visibility of up to 90 feet, the waters around Aruba
are excellent for snorkeling and diving. In fact, Aruba is
known as one of the wreck diving capitals of the Caribbean.
Advanced and novice divers alike will find plenty to occupy
their time, as many of the most popular sites—including
some interesting shipwrecks—are found in shallow waters
ranging from 30 to 60 feet. Coral reefs covered with sensu-
ously waving sea fans and eerie giant sponge tubes attract
a colorful menagerie of sea life, including gliding manta
rays, curious sea turtles, shy octopuses, and fish from grunts
to groupers. Marine preservation is a priority on Aruba,
and regulations by the Conference on International Trade
in Endangered Species make it unlawful to remove coral,
conch, and other marine life from the water.

In 2010 the Aruba Marine Park Foundation was established
to protect the island's reefs and waters. It's a not-for-profit
government organization, and they have been busy study-
ing and defining the parameters that will best serve the
island. One big issue they are tackling is the invasion of
the non-native lionfish that threatens reefs throughout the
Caribbean. If you spot a lionfish, report it to their organization, and do not touch it. The venom is poisonous and
the sting very painful.

8

Day Sail operators offer snorkeling, but it's usually coupled
with an open bar and loud music, making the trip the focus
more than what you see underwater, though almost all of
them stop at the famous *Antilla* shipwreck just offshore
which provides a rare treat for snorkelers to be able to
view a wreck typically only divers would be able to access.
Some dive operators also allow snorkelers to tag along with
divers on a trip for a lower fee as well.

MAJOR WEST-SIDE DIVE SITES

Antilla **Wreck.** This German freighter, which sank off the
northwest coast near Malmok Beach, is popular with both
divers and snorkelers. Some outfits also offer SNUBA,
which will allow you to get a bit closer to the wreck when
you are not certified to dive. When Germany declared war

DID YOU KNOW?

Whereas windsurfers stand on a large board connected to a sail, kitesurfers ride a much smaller board and are propelled by a kite that flies high in the air.

Diving one of Aruba's many wrecks

on the Netherlands in 1940 during World War II it was stationed off the coast where it still is now. The captain chose to sink the ship on purpose before Aruban officials could board and seize it. The 400-foot-long vessel—referred to by locals as "the ghost ship"— broke into two distinct halves. It has large compartments, and you can climb into the captain's bathtub, which sits beside the wreck, for a unique photo op. Lobster, angelfish, yellowtail, and other fish swim about the wreck, which is blanketed by giant tube sponges and coral.

Airplane Wrecks. Two planes purposely scuttled to create a new dive site are still somewhat intact around Renaissance Private Island. You must do a drift dive to see them; they broke apart somewhat after Hurricane Lenny caused big swells in the area.

Black Beach. The clear waters just off this beach are dotted with sea fans. The area takes its name from the rounded black stones lining the shore. It's the only bay on the island's north coast sheltered from thunderous waves, making it a safe spot for diving.

Californian **Wreck.** Although this steamer is submerged at a depth that's perfect for underwater photography, this site is safe only for advanced divers; the currents here are strong, and the waters are dangerously choppy. This wreck is what the famous lighthouse is named for.

Malmok Reef (*Debbie II* Wreck). Lobsters and stingrays are among the highlights at this bottom reef adorned by giant green, orange, and purple barrel sponges as well as leaf and brain coral. From here you can spot the *Debbie II*, a 120-foot barge that sank in 1992.

Pedernales Wreck. During World War II, this oil tanker was torpedoed by a German submarine. The U.S. military cut out the damaged centerpiece, towed the two remaining pieces to the States, and welded them together into a smaller vessel that eventually transported troops during the invasion of Normandy. The section that was left behind in shallow water is now surrounded by coral formations, making this a good site for novice divers. The ship's cabins, washbasins, and pipelines are exposed. The area teems with grouper and angelfish. It's also a good site for snorkelers since it's easily visible from the shallows.

Tugboat Wreck. Spotted eagle rays and stingrays are sometimes observed at this shipwreck at the foot of Harbour Reef, which is one of Aruba's most popular. Spectacular formations of brain, sheet, and star coral blanket the path to the wreck, which is inhabited by several bright-green moray eels.

EAST-SIDE DIVE SITES

DePalm Island. A must-do for fabulous snorkeling with giant neon blue smiling parrotfish that look like animated characters. Secluded behind clusters of mangroves, the reef system stretches all the way to Oranjestad. You can get close enough to touch the nurse sharks that sleep tucked into reef crevices during the day. But it's more than a dive and snorkeling destination. It's really a tourist attraction that appeals to all ages and offers a plethora of activities.

Jane C. Wreck. This 200-foot freighter, lodged in an almost vertical position at a depth of 90 feet, is near the coral reef west of De Palm Island. Night diving is exciting here, as the polyps emerge from the corals that grow profusely on the steel plates of the decks and cabins. Soft corals and sea fans are also abundant in the area. The current is strong, and this is for advanced divers only.

Punta Basora. This narrow reef stretches far into the sea off the island's easternmost point. On calm days you'll see eagle rays, stingrays, barracudas, and hammerhead sharks, as well as hawksbill and loggerhead turtles.

The Wall. From May to August, green sea turtles intent on laying their eggs abound at this steep-walled reef. You'll also spot groupers and burrfish swimming nearby. Close to shore, massive sheet corals are plentiful; in the upper part of the reef are colorful varieties such as black coral, star coral, and flower coral. Flitting about are brilliant damselfish, rock beauties, and porgies.

RECOMMENDED DIVE OPERATORS

★ Fodor'sChoice **Aruba Watersports Center—Arusun Snorkel.** This FAMILY family-run, full-service water sports outfitter is right on Palm Beach, offering a comprehensive variety of adventures including diving and snorkeling trips, but also Wave runners, tubing, Hobie Cat sailing, stand-up paddleboarding, kayaking, wakeboard, and waterskiing. Snorkeling trips aboard the *Arusun* are for small groups, and the boat goes to spots others don't, including the *Pederanles* wreck. ✉ *L.G. Smith Blvd. 81B, Palm Beach ✛ Between Barcelo and Hilton resorts* ☎ *297/586–6613* ⊕ *www.arubawatersportscenter.com* 🖥 *From $20.*

Dive Aruba. Resort courses, certification courses, and trips to interesting shipwrecks make Dive Aruba worth checking out. The outfitter only offers small group dives. ✉ *Wilhelminastraat 8, Oranjestad* ☎ *297/582–7337* ⊕ *www.divearuba.com.*

★ Fodor'sChoice **Full Throttle Tours.** This wild and crazy thrill ride aboard a rigid, inflatable speedboat takes snorkelers to two gorgeous spots that no other operators visit. You leave from downtown and tear up the coast to Arashi Reef for your first stop, and then take another roaring jaunt all the way to Mangel Halto for more terrific snorkeling. Snacks and drinks are included. The boat only seats ten people, so reserve ahead (you'll also pay less if you reserve online). ⚠ This tour is great fun, but it can be bouncy, so it's not recommended for pregnant women or those with chronic back and neck issues. ✉ *Renaissance Marina, Oranjestad ✛ Look for their sign at entrance to the pier* ☎ *297/741–8570* ⊕ *www.fullthrottletoursaruba.com* 🖥 *From $52.*

★ Fodor'sChoice **JADS Dive Center.** JP Fang has moved his dive operation out to Baby Beach in San Nicolas, where he has built an entire complex around the old Esso Social Club. There is a dive shop and snorkel equipment rentals; the company offers charters to experienced divers, but also specializes in first-rate instruction for beginners. After a briefing, you head to Mangel Halto nearby for an easy shore dive that takes you to a little ship they scuttled to make an artificial reef. The complex also has washroom facilities, a playground, an outdoor shower, and a full beach bar-diner that has great local food, specialty cocktails, and sometimes live music. A new bar next to an infinity pool is under development there, too. ■TIP→ One dive instructor sells unique handmade jewelry made from lionfish skin in the dive shop for a cool souvenir and helps rid the environment of these destructive fish. ⊠ *Seroe Colorado 245E, Seroe Colorado* ☎ *297/584–6070* ⊕ *www.jadsaruba.com* ⊠ *From $55.*

Native Divers Aruba. A small, personal operation, Native Divers Aruba specializes in PADI open-water courses. Ten different certification options include specialties like Multilevel Diver, Search & Recovery Diver, and Underwater Naturalist. Their boat schedule is also flexible, and it's easy to tailor instruction to your specific needs. They also allow snorkelers to tag along and provide all the necessary equipment. ⊠ *Marriott Surf Club, Palm Beach* ☎ *297/586–4763* ⊕ *www.nativedivers.com* ⊠ *Snorkel from $25, dive from $80.*

S.E. Aruba Fly 'n Dive. One of the island's oldest diving operators, S.E. Aruba Fly 'n Dive offers a full range of PADI courses as well as many specialty courses like Nitrox Diver, Wreck Diver, and Deep Diver. They can also instruct you in rescue techniques and becoming an underwater naturalist. ⊠ *L. G. Smith Blvd. 1A, Oranjestad* ☎ *297/588–1150* ⊕ *www.se-aruba.com* ⊠ *From $60.*

Unique Sports of Aruba. Diving is the specialty here, with scads of one- or two-tank dives scheduled weekly on a fleet of three dive boats. The staff teach beginner resort courses as well as a wide range of PADI courses, including dive master and rescue. All trips depart from DePalm Pier, between the Riu and Hilton resorts. ⊠ *De Palm Pier, Palm Beach* ☎ *297/594–7250* ⊕ *www.uniquesportsaruba. com* ⊠ *From $150.*

8

SKYDIVING

★ **Fodor'sChoice SkyDive Aruba.** There's nothing like the adrenaline rush when you are forced to jump out of a perfectly good airplane at 10,000 feet because you are attached to your instructor. You have no choice but to free-fall at 120 mph toward the island for 35 seconds until your chute

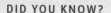

opens, and then your downward journey has you floating to the sand in a little over five minutes. Afterward you can purchase a video of your courageous leap. Group discounts are available. ⊠ *Malmok Beach, Malmokweg* ☎ *297/735–0654* ⊕ *www.skydivearuba.com* ☜ *From $250.*

SUBMARINE EXCURSIONS

Atlantis Submarines. Enjoy the deep without getting wet in a real U.S. Coast Guard–approved submarine with *Atlantis* , run by De Palm Tours and operating on the island for over 25 years. The underwater reefs are teeming with marine life, and the 65-foot air-conditioned sub takes up to 48 passengers for a two-hour tour 95 to 150 feet below the surface along Barcadera. The company also owns the *Seaworld Explorer,* a semisubmersible that allows you to sit and view Aruba's marine habitat from five feet below the surface. (Children must be a minimum of 36 inches in height and four years old.) ⊠ *Renaissance Marina, L. G. Smith Blvd. 82, Oranjestad* ☎ *297/583–6090* ⊕ *www.depalmtours.com/ atlantis-submarines-expedition* ☜ *From $105.*

TENNIS

Aruba Racquet Club. Aruba's winds make tennis a challenge even if you have the best of backhands. Although visitors can make arrangements to play at the resorts, priority goes to guests. Some private tennis clubs can also accommodate you, or you can try the facilities at the Aruba Racquet Club. Host to a variety of international tournaments, the club has eight courts (six lighted), as well as a swimming pool, an aerobics center, and a restaurant. ⊠ *Rooisanto 21, Palm Beach* ☎ *297/586–0215* ⊕ *www.arc.aw* ☜ *Lessons from $45.*

WINDSURFING AND KITEBOARDING

Aruba has all it takes for windsurfing: trade winds that average 15 knots year-round (peaking May–July), a sunny climate, and perfect azure-blue waters. With a few lessons from a certified instructor, even novices will be jibing in no time. The southwestern coast's tranquil waters make it ideal for both beginners and intermediates, as the winds are steady but sudden gusts rare. Experts will find the waters of the Atlantic, especially around Grapefield and Boca Grandi beaches, more challenging; winds are fierce and often shift without warning. Some hotels include windsurfing in their water-sports packages, and most operators can help you arrange complete windsurfing vacations.

Kiteboarding has almost overtaken windsurfing as the island's most popular wind sport to learn these days. The sport involves gliding on and above the water on a small surfboard or wakeboard while hooked up to an inflatable kite. Windsurfing experience helps, and practice time on the beach is essential, but these are different sports. You can watch the colorful kites flying all around Fisherman's Huts Beach, where boarders practice and give lessons. Pros will tell you that kiteboarding takes longer to learn, so carve out at least four hours for your first lesson on the beach. Nevertheless, once you learn how, it's easier to learn new tricks while kiteboarding.

Every July sees the Hi-Winds Pro-Am Windsurfing Competition, attracting professionals and amateurs from around the world. There are divisions for women, men, juniors, masters, and grand masters. Disciplines include slalom, course racing, long distance, and freestyle. The event attarcts visitors and competitors from all over the world and has become one big beach party with entertainment and additional events that go day and night.

★ FodorśChoice **Aruba Active Vacations.** Located near Fishermen's
FAMILY Huts—the best spot on the island for optimum wind and wave conditions—this operation has been the go-to for many years as THE best place to learn windsurfing, and more recently kiteboarding. Local alums of their school include world-class competitors like Women's Windsurf Champion Sarah-Quita Offringa, and their expert instructors ensure even first-timers are riding the waves in no time. They also offer mountain biking and stand-up paddleboarding, and they are the only outfit on the island that does "blokarting"—sail-powered land carting. ⊠ *L.G. Smith Blvd. 486, Palm Beach ✛ Near Fisherman's Huts* ☎ *297/586–0989* ⊕ *www.aruba-active-vacations.com* 🖃 *From $50.*

FAMILY **Vela Aruba.** All kinds of sporty fun-in-the-sun options are available at this fun and funky kiosk in the sand, including professional windsurfing and kiteboarding lessons. You can rent sea kayaks and stand-up paddleboards (and take lessons in both; instructors even offer yoga on stand-up paddleboard). But if you'd rather plant your feet in the sand to do your yoga, you can do that, too. ⊠ *L.G. Smith Blvd. 101, Palm Beach ✛ Between the Aruba Marriott and the Ritz-Carlton* ☎ *297/586–3735* ⊕ *www.velaaruba.com* 🖃 *Rentals from $35, lessons from $60.*

SHOPPING AND SPAS

SHOPPING CAN BE GOOD ON Aruba. Although stores on the island often use the tagline "duty-free," the word "prices" is usually printed underneath in much smaller letters. The only real duty-free shopping is in the departures area of the airport. (Passengers bound for the United States should be sure to shop before proceeding through U.S. customs in Aruba.) Downtown stores do have very low sales tax, though, and they offer some excellent bargains on high-end luxury items like gold, silver, gems, and high-end watches. Major credit cards are welcome everywhere, as are U.S. dollars.

Aruba's souvenir and crafts stores are full of Dutch porcelains and figurines, as befits the island's heritage. Dutch cheese is a good buy, as are hand-embroidered linens and any products made from the native aloe vera plant—sunburn cream, face masks, or skin refreshers found in the many official Aruba Aloe stores. Local arts and crafts run toward wood carvings and earthenware emblazoned with "Aruba: One Happy Island" and the like, but there are many shops with unique Aruban items like designer wear and fancy flip-flops and artwork if you know where to look. And new arts foundations like Cosecha in Oranjestad and San Nicolas offer up only certifiably authentic, high-quality arts and crafts made in Aruba by talented local artisans. Don't try to bargain unless you are at a flea market or stall. Arubans consider it rude to haggle, despite what you may hear to the contrary.

HOW AND WHEN

A good way to preview the shops and malls in downtown Oranjestad is to hop aboard the free trolley that loops the downtown area. There are some interesting new offerings in the back streets, including big-name brand megastores wedged in between smaller mom-and-pop shops. Also the smaller malls along the strip like the Village Square have some unique artisan shops, as does Paseo Herencia, whose courtyard is the scene of nightly entertainment called "the Waltzing Waters."

There is late-night shopping in two locations. The first, in downtown Oranjestad at Renaissance Mall—a multilevel indoor/outdoor complex—stays open until 8 pm, and shops in the modern, multilevel indoor shopping mall off the high-rise strip—Palm Beach Plaza—stay open until 10 pm. Many of the shops around Paseo Herencia also stay open late in high season. A few other shops that stay open late can be found in Alhambra Mall as well. And most resorts have their own shops.

ORANJESTAD AND ENVIRONS

Oranjestad's original "Main Street" (behind the Renaissance Marina Resort) had been neglected since most cruise passengers preferred to stick to the front street near the marina, where many high-end shops and open-market souvenir stalls are. Nevertheless, a massive renovation of the entire downtown region has breathed new life into the back streets, adding pedestrian-only stretches, compact malls, and open resting areas. A free eco-trolley now loops throughout downtown, allowing you to hop on and off to shop and stroll. Stores selling fashions, souvenirs, specialty items, sporting goods, and cosmetics can all be found on this renewed street, along with plenty of cafés, snack spots, and outdoor terraces, where you can catch your breath between retail therapy jaunts.

CIGARS

Cigar Emporium. The Cubans come straight from the climate-controlled humidor at Cigar Emporium. Choose from Cohiba, Montecristo, Romeo y Julieta, Partagas, and more. ⊠ *Renaissance Mall, L.G. Smith Blvd. 82, Oranjestad* ☏ *297/582–5479.*

CLOTHING AND ACCESSORIES

★ Fodor'sChoice **Gucci.** What's in a name? When the name is Gucci, you know it's always trendsetting top quality. The sophisticated store offers fashions for men and women as well as their distinctive luxury shoes, handbags, leather goods, eyewear, and accessories. ⊠ *Renaissance Mall, L. G. Smith Blvd. 82, Oranjestad* ☏ *297/583–3952* ⊕ *www. shoprenaissancearuba.com.*

★ Fodor'sChoice **Mango.** A complete makeover to match the downtown restoration has turned this popular Spanish chain outlet into a megastore that now dominates the block along the trolley tracks on Main Street. It offers multiple levels of air-condtioned, fashion-forward shopping for all ages. Plus-size fashions are available, too. It's as popular with the locals as it is with visitors. ⊠ *Caya Betico Croes 9, Oranjestad* ☏ *297/582–9800.*

Tommy Hilfiger. The activewear sold at Tommy Hilfiger makes this a great stop for a vacation wardrobe. A Tommy Jeans store is also there. There are also stores in the Renaissance Mall and Paseo Herencia Mall on the high-rise resort

9

strip. ⊠ *Royal Plaza Mall, L. G. Smith Blvd. 94, Oranjestad* ☎ *297/583–8548* ⊕ *global.tommy.com.*

DUTY-FREE STORES

Dufry. No doubt you've seen this brand of duty-free stores in airports all over the world, but don't expect to see the same duty-free items like tobacco and spirits in this one, and the prices are not completely duty-free. What you will find are great bargains on cosmetics, perfumes, jewelery, and accessories from such brands as Carolina Herrara, Calvin Klein, Armani, Montblanc, and more. And there's always some kind of major sale on something of good quality going on there. There's another outlet in Royal Plaza Mall. ⊠ *G.F. Betico Croes 29, Oranjestad* ☎ *297/582–2790* ⊕ *www.dufry.com.*

ELECTRONICS

★ Fodor'sChoice **Boolchand's Digital World.** Family-run Boolchand's began in the 1930s and has since become a major retail institution throughout the Caribbean; they opened their first shop on Aruba in 1974. Today, their downtown "Digital World" is your one-stop-shop to get a high-tech fix at seriously low prices. Top-quality merchandise by major brands includes the latest in computers, cameras, tech accessories, as well as quality watches and Pandora jewelry. ⊠ *Havenstraat 25, Oranjestad* ☎ *297/583–0147* ⊕ *www.boolchand.com.*

FOOD

Ling & Sons IGA Super Center. Always a family-owned and family-operated grocery company, Ling and Sons adopted the IGA-brand supermarket style with all the goods you would expect in an IGA back home. In addition to a wide variety of foods, there's a bakery, a deli, a butcher shop, and a well-stocked "liquortique." You can also order your groceries online to be delivered to your hotel room. Ask about their VIP card for discounts. ⊠ *Schotlandstraat 41, Oranjestad* ☎ *297/521–2370* ⊕ *www.lingandsons.com.*

GIFTS AND SOUVENIRS

★ **Fodor's Choice The Mask—Mopa Mopa Art.** These shops specialize in original masks and crafty items called mopa mopa art. Originating with the Quillacingas people of Ecuador and Colombia, the art is made from the bud of the mopa mopa tree, boiled down into a resin, colored with dyes, and applied to carved mahogany and other woods like cedar. Masks, jewelry boxes, coasters, whimsical animal figurines, and more make wonderfully unique gifts and souvenirs. The masks are also believed to ward off evil spirits. Find them in Paseo Herencia Mall, Royal Plaza Mall, and Renaissance Marketplace. You can also buy works online ⊠ *Renaissance Marketplace, L.G. Smith Blvd. 9, Oranjestad* ☎ *297/586–2900* ⊕ *www.mopamopa.com.*

JEWELRY

★ **Fodor's Choice Colombian Emeralds International.** A trusted international jewelry dealer specializing in emeralds, this outlet also has a top-notch selection of diamonds, sapphire, tanzanite, rubies, ammolite, pearls, gold, semiprecious gems, luxury watches, and more at very competitive prices. A highly professional and knowledgeable staff adds to their credibility. ⊠ *Renaissance Mall, L.G. Smith Blvd. 82, Oranjestad* ☎ *297/583–6238* ⊕ *www.colombianemeralds.com.*

★ **Fodor's Choice Diamonds International.** One of the pioneer diamond retailers in the Caribbean with over 125 stores throughout the chain, the Aruba outlet has been operating in the same spot since 1997, and you can't miss the mammoth store as soon as you step off a cruise ship. The company is well-known for their expertise, selection, quality, and competitive prices on diamonds, and they also sell high-end timepieces. The founders of Diamonds International are both graduates of the Gemological Institute of America. You'll find smaller outlets in many of the island's top resorts. ⊠ *L.G. Smith Blvd. 17, Oranjestad* ☎ *800/515–3935* ⊕ *www.diamondsinternational.com.*

Gandelman Jewelers. Established in 1936, this family-run store is one of the island's premier jewelers. It's also Aruba's official Rolex retailer and the exclusive agent for names like Cartier (the only official retailer on the island), Patek Philippe, and David Yurman. There are two other stores on Aruba in the Aruba Marriott and the Aruba Hyatt Regency in addition to this flagship. ⊠ *Renaissance Mall, L. G. Smith Blvd. 82, Oranjestad* ☎ *297/529–9000* ⊕ *www.gandelman.net.*

9

★ Fodor'sChoice **Kay's Fine Jewelry.** Kay's family-run emporium is a well-known Aruba fixture on the fine-jewelry scene, and their designs have won awards. Exquisite settings featuring white and colored diamonds are their claim to fame, and they also have a fine selection of precious gems and brand-name timepieces. ✉ *Westraat 8, Oranjestad* ☎ *297/598–9978* ⊕ *www.kaysfinejewelry.com/aruba_downtown_jewelry_store.php.*

Little Switzerland. With four stores on the island—mostly in high-rise resorts and the original location in downtown Royal Plaza Mall—these well-known outlets specialize in designer jewelry and upscale timepieces by big-name designers like TAGHeuer, David Yurman, Breitling, Roberto Coin, Chopard, Pandora, Tiffany & Co., Cartier Movado, Omega, and John Hardy. ✉ *Royal Plaza Mall, L.G. Smith Blvd. 94, Oranjestad* ☎ *284/809–5560* ⊕ *www.littleswitzerland.com.*

MALLS AND MARKETPLACES

★ Fodor'sChoice **Renaissance Mall.** Upscale, name-brand fashion and luxury brands of perfume, cosmetics, leather goods are what you'll find in the array of 60 stores spanning two floors in this mall located within and underneath the Renaissance Marina Resort. You'll also find specialty items like cigars and designer shoes plus high-end gold, silver, diamonds, and quality jewelry at low-duty and no-tax prices. Cafés and high-end dining, plus a casino and spa round out the offerings. Shopping until 8 pm daily. ✉ *Renaissance Marina Resort, L.G. Smith Blvd. 82, Oranjestad* ☎ *297/582–4622* ⊕ *www.shoprenaissancearuba.com.*

★ Fodor'sChoice **Renaissance Marketplace.** Really more of a dining and gathering spot along the marina than a shopping complex, this is a lively alfresco mall with a few souvenir shops, specialty stores, and a no-name gallery with gorgeous handcrafted sea glass creations made by Gaby, a well-known local artist better known by her brand, Aruba's Hands by Gaby. There is also a modern cinema. But mostly it's full of eclectic dining emporiums and trendy cafés. There's live music most nights in the common square. ✉ *L.G. Smith Blvd. 9, Oranjestad* ⊕ *www.shoprenaissancearuba.com.*

Royal Plaza Mall. It's impossible to miss this gorgeous colonial-style, cotton-candy-colored building with the big gold dome gracing the front street along the marina. It's one of the most photographed in Oranjestad. Three levels of

Beyond T-Shirts and Key Chains

You can't go wrong with baseball caps, refrigerator magnets, beer mugs, sweatshirts, T-shirts, key chains, and other local logo merchandise. You won't go broke buying these items, either. But do try to look for items actually made on Aruba rather than imported from China. Seek out the local market near the cruise ship terminal for more items made locally; look for the giant red chair.

Budget for a major purchase. If souvenirs are all about keeping the memories alive in the long haul, plan ahead to shop for something really special—a work of art, a rug or something else handcrafted, or a major accessory for your home. One major purchase will stay with you far longer than a dozen tourist trinkets.

Add to your collection. Whether antiques, used books, salt-and-pepper shakers, or ceramic frogs are your thing, start looking in the first day or two. Chances are you'll want to scout around and then go back to some of the first shops you visited before you hand over your credit card.

Get guarantees in writing. Is the vendor making promises? Ask him or her to put them in writing.

Anticipate a shopping spree. Buy a reusable bag while on island, maybe more than one ... as Aruba has banned all retail stores from supplying plastic bags for the good of the environment since Jan. 2016. Pack a large tote bag in your suitcase in case you need extra space. If you think you might buy breakables, include a length of bubble wrap. Don't fill your suitcase to bursting before you leave home. Or include some old clothing that you can leave behind to make room for new acquisitions.

Know before you go. Study prices at home on items you might consider buying while you're away. Otherwise you won't recognize a bargain when you see one.

Plastic, please. Especially if your purchase is pricey and you're looking for authenticity, it's always smart to pay with a credit card. If a problem arises later and the merchant can't or won't resolve it, the credit-card company may help you out.

9

shops—indoor and outdoor—make up this artsy arcade full of small boutiques, cigar shops, designer clothing outlets, gift and jewelery stores, and souvenir kiosks. Great dining and bars within as well. ⊠ *L.G. Smith Blvd. 94, Oranjestad* ☎ *297/588–0351.*

ARUBA TRADING
COMPANY

Shopping That Gives Back

American expat Jodi Tobman moved to Aruba in the 1990s. Her chain of unique retail stores is well-known among local and repeat visitors as having some of the most interesting finds on the island. But her stores are also different because they are part of a community give-back program called Tikkun Olam, which loosely translates to "repair the world" in Hebrew.

The stores that participate in this program give back a percentage of their sales to community programs. At point of purchase, customers choose from a Community Menu, earmarking their choice for that store to donate to on their behalf. From Alzheimer's and cancer support to autism, education for children, elder support, abused women, the arts, and even youth sports, each store has its own menu of foundations it supports.

Seeking out and patronizing these shops is worth it not only for the good feeling you get knowing you are giving back to your host island community in some way, but also for the wares they sell. Tobman travels the globe seeking out unique products to stock the stores, always with an eye toward handcrafted or sustainable or arty concepts. Stores that participate are The Juggling Fish, The Lazy Lizard, T.H. Palm and Co., and A Taste of Aruba. Stores are located in both the high-rise and low-rise hotel sector along both Palm and Eagle beaches, and the items they stock run the gamut from avant-garde arty gifts and souvenirs to high-quality swimwear and apparel and gifts for the home.

Locals often seek out these stores to buy gifts for special occasions, knowing that their purchase goes toward community support, and the gorgeous items always on offer make fabulous souvenirs for the folks back home, too.

PERFUMES AND COSMETICS

Penha, Dufry, Little Switzerland, and Maggy's are all known for their extensive fragrance offerings.

Aruba Trading Company. Established in 1933 and located in the gorgeous Dutch colonial structure known as *La Casa Amarilla* (The Yellow House) in downtown Oranjestad, this shop specializes in fine perfumes and high-end cosmetics, but it also sells wine and liquor. ⊠ *Caya G.F. Betico Croes 12, Oranjestad* ☎ *297/582–2602* ⊕ *www.arubatrading.com.*

Penha. Originating in Curaçao in 1865, Penha has branched out throughout the Caribbean and has eight stores on Aruba. The largest is right next to the Renaissance Marina Hotel. The store is particularly known for good prices on high-end perfumes, cosmetics, skin-care products, eyewear, and fashions. You'll find brand names such as MAC, Lancôme, Estée Lauder, Clinique, Chanel, Dior, Montblanc, and Victoria's Secret to name just a few. ⊠ *Caya G.F. Betico Croes 11/13, Oranjestad* ☎ *297/582–4160, 297/582–4161* ⊕ *www.jlpenha.com.*

SPAS

★ Fodor'sChoice **Okeanos Spa.** The full-service spa at the Renaissance Marina Hotel is well-equipped to help you relax to the max, but the incredible seaside palapa cove on private Renaissance Island is the best venue for a relaxing massage or treatment. It's accessible by free water taxi when you book a treatment, and your purchase also gains you access to the stellar protected coves and white-sand beaches. Access to the island is otherwise limited to Renaissance guests. There is a beach bar and a full-service restaurant on-site, so you can make an entire blissful day of it. ⊠ *Renaissance Aruba Resort & Casino, L.G. Smith Blvd. 82, Oranjestad* ☎ *297/583–6000* ⊕ *www.renaissancearubaspa.com.*

DRUIF

FOOD

Kong Hing Supercentre. This clean, orderly supermarket within easy walking distance of Druif Beach stocks all the typical grocery store staples, including fresh produce, meats, canned goods, baked goods, and a wide selection of beer, wine, and liquor. ⊠ *L. G. Smith Blvd. 152, Druif* ☎ *297/582–5545.*

MALLS AND MARKETPLACES

★ Fodor'sChoice **Alhambra Mall.** There's an eclectic array of shops and dining in the Alhambra Mall with the casino as its focal point. Dotted with designer retail stores and souvenir shops and a full-service market and deli, the alfresco mall also has fast-food outlets like Juan Valdez Coffee Shop, Baskin-Robbins, and Subway. Fusions Wine & Tapas Bar, We'r Cuba and Twist of Flavors restaurant round out the dining options. There's also a small full-service spa. Stores are open late. The casino is open until the wee hours. ⊠ *L.G. Smith Blvd. 47, Druif.*

SPAS

Indulgence by the Sea Spa. The spa-salon serving Divi Aruba and Tamarijn all-inclusives offers a wide range of premium services. Begin your journey to relaxation with a rose-filled pure essential oil footbath, cold cucumbers for the eyes, and a lavender heat wrap. Products are organic and natural—all handpicked and tested by the owner. A full range of massages includes a couples sea escape in a private cabana. The spa portion is at Divi Aruba, and the salon that specializes in bridal parties for special-occasion hair and makeup is at Tamarijn. They also service Divi Dutch Village and Divi Golf Village. ⊠ *J. E. Irausquin Blvd. 45, Druif* ☎ *297/583–0083* ⊕ *spaaruba.com.*

EAGLE BEACH

FOOD

★ Fodor's Choice **SuperFood Plaza.** So much more than a grocery store, it's a massive emporium that offers all kinds of extras beyond just fresh food and other staples; it's more like a small department store. Beyond a huge fresh produce section, fresh fish and seafood market, bakery and deli section, there's also a café, a drugstore, and even a toy store on-site. It's truly a one-stop for all your needs. ⊠ *Bubali 141-A, Eagle Beach* ☎ *297/522–2000* ⊕ *www.superfoodaruba.com.*

PALM BEACH AND NOORD

CIGARS

★ Fodor's Choice **Aruhiba Cigars.** Look for the big red windmill just off Palm Beach to find this little factory kiosk outlet where the owner hand-rolls quality cigars from tobacco grown on Aruba. Aruhibas have become as popular as Cubans with locals on the island, and in terms of quality they are seriously on par with those from Havana. They are also a legal option for visitors seeking cigars to bring back to the United States. ⊠ *Historic Red Windmill, J.E. Irausquin Blvd. 330* ⊹ *Near The Mill Resort* ☎ *297/567–1599* ⊕ *www.aruhibacigars.com.*

CLOTHING AND ACCESSORIES

★ Fodor'sChoice **The Lazy Lizard.** Fun and trendy beachwear and resort fashions along with accessories like fancy flip-flops, sandals, Aruba-inspired T-shirts, and totes for the whole family. There are souvenirs as well. A sister store is in the Alhambra Mall and is part of The Salamander Group, where a portion of the proceeds go to local charities. ⊠ *South Beach Centre, Palm Beach 55, Palm Beach* ⊹ *Next to the Hard Rock Cafe* ☎ *297/592–7087* ⊕ *www. thelazylizard.com.*

GIFTS AND SOUVENIRS

A Taste of Aruba. This small sundry store has a surprisingly eclectic selection of made-in-Aruba art, locally sourced crafts, and special souvenirs like fancy hand-painted hats. You can also pick up a great little selection of Caribbean-inspired gifts and jewelry. ⊠ *South Beach Centre, Palm Beach* ☎ *297/592–7801.*

★ Fodor'sChoice **The Juggling Fish.** This whimsical shop just off the sand is really two separate entities. One side is Juggling Fish Swimwear, a comprehensive selection of quality bathing suits and beach accessories for the entire family, and the other side is dedicated to a panapoly of creative and unique gifts and souvenirs including avant-garde jewelry and handcrafted items. The staff is warm and friendly, and a portion of all purchases goes to community programs and charities. ⊠ *Playa Linda Beach Resort, Palm Beach* ☎ *297/586–4999* ⊕ *www.thejugglingfish.com.*

★ Fodor'sChoice **T.H. Palm & Company.** With an eclectic collection of upscale and exclusive items curated from all over the world by the owner, this unique boutique offers everything from top-line fashions for men and women, including footwear, handcrafted jewelry, and accessories, to art deco items for the home and novelty gifts for pets. It's a very popular spot for locals to buy gifts as well as for visitors to buy one-of-a-kind souvenirs. A portion of all purchases goes to the community through a special give-back program. ⊠ *J. E. Irausquin Blvd. 87, Palm Beach* ☎ *297/586–6898.*

JEWELRY

★ **Fodor'sChoice** **Shiva's Gold and Gems.** A reputable family-run business with shops throughout the Caribbean, this Palm Beach Plaza location saves shoppers from heading to Oranjestad for the type of top-quality diamonds and jewelry downtown is famous for (though there is a location downtown as well). Luxury watches, precious gems, gold, silver, and more are first-rate here, and this is the only store on Aruba that belongs to the Leading Jewelers of the World, which has fewer than 100 retail members. ✉ *Palm Beach Plaza, L.G. Smith 95, Palm Beach* ☎ *297/586–2586* ⊕ *www.shivasjewlers.com.*

MALLS AND MARKETPLACES

★ **Fodor'sChoice** **Palm Beach Plaza.** Aruba's most modern multi-story mall has three floors of shops offering fashion, tech, electronics, jewelry, souvenirs, and more. Entertainment includes, glow-in-the-dark bowling, a modern video arcade, a sports bar, and the main floor indoor courtyard is often used for local festivals and events like fashion shows. Dining includes a food court and lots of stand-alone restaurants and bars, and there are also modern air-conditioned cinemas and a spa within. Free Wi-Fi is a bonus, too. ✉ *L.G. Smith Boulevard 95, Palm Beach* ☎ *297/586–0045* ⊕ *www. palmbeachplaza.com.*

★ **Fodor'sChoice** **Paseo Herencia.** A gorgeous, old-fashioned colonial-style courtyard and clock tower encases souvenir and specialty shops, cinemas, dining spots, cafés, and bars in this low-rise alfresco mall just off Palm Beach. Famous for its "liquid fireworks" shows when four times a night neon-lit water fountains waltz to music in a choreographed dance. Visitors can enjoy it for free from an outdoor amphitheater where many cultural events take place, and there's an Aruban walk of fame there. There's also a fancy carousel for children. A must visit—if not for the shopping—then for the water show. ✉ *J.E. Irausquin Blvd. 382, Palm Beach* ☎ *297/586–6533* ⊕ *www.paseoherencia.com.*

FAMILY

9

PERFUMES AND COSMETICS

★ **Fodor'sChoice** **Maggy's Perfumery and Salon.** A true local success story, this is one of the four locations in a local chain that began as a small salon in San Nicolas and evolved into a major perfumery with salons and stores. Though the original Maggy has since passed, the business she began in

Many Aruba resorts have thier own spas providing body treatments and massages.

1969 is still going strong with her daughter at the helm and many family members still running the business. Quality perfumes and beauty products, as well as health and beauty care services are all to be found at all outlets. ⊠ *Paseo Herencia, L. G. Smith Blvd. 382, Palm Beach* ☎ *297/586–2113.*

SPAS

★ **Fodor's**Choice **Eforea Spa.** Hilton's new answer to Zen incarnate, the soothing white seafront building beckons you to enter a world of relaxing signature "journeys" in a Japanese-inspired enclave. Treatments include both the typical and avant-garde, and there are options for both women and men, as well as special seaside massages for couples. There's also a stellar water circuit and full-service beauty salon on-site. ⊠ *Hilton Aruba Resort, J.E.Irausquin Blvd.81, Palm Beach* ☎ *297/526–6052* ⊕ *www.hiltonarubacaribbean.hilton.com.*

★ **Fodor's**Choice **Mandara Spa.** Aruba Marriott's Mandara Spa was created along a Balinese theme and offers specialty Indonesian-style treatments that incorporate the *boreh* (a traditional warm healing pack of special spices) followed by an Aruba-inspired wrap using local aloe and cucumber. The menu also lists a wide variety of skin and body treatments for both women and men, and there's a full-service hair and nail salon, ideal for a wedding party. Honeymooners and couples will appreciate special packages that include private couple's treatment rooms, extra-large whirlpool baths, and Vichy showers. ⊠ *Aruba Marriott Resort & Stellaris Casino, L. G. Smith Blvd. 101, Palm Beach* ☎ *297/520–6750* ⊕ *hwww.mandaraspa.com.*

New Image Spa. A full-service spa and beauty center in the Barcelo Resort offers a comprehensive range of services. Beyond the typical spa menu of massages, facials, wraps, and mani-pedis, you can also get foot reflexology, detox-ification, permanent makeup, cosmetology, hair removal, injectables, or simple hairdressing. The concept of all treat-ments is to utilize organic and natural products whenever possible. ⊠ *Barcelo Resort, J.E. Irausquin 83, Palm Beach* ☎ *297/582–2288* ⊕ *www.newimagearuba.com.*

The Spa at Tierra del Sol. Tierra del Sol's luxury villa and home rentals are typically the visiting-celebrity choice, and their Robert Trent Jones II–designed golf course is where serious golfers play. So it's no surprise that this spa blends into the entire upscale luxury scene here perfectly. One highlight is the pampering private-couples whirlpool where romantics can canoodle with champagne in peace. They also have an interesting sea-sand detox skin treatment. But most come here for the high-end massages, wraps, scrubs, and skin treatments, and there is also a full hair and nail care salon. Spa guests are welcome to use the fitness center and lounge by the cliffside pool looking out at the California Lighthouse. ⊠ *Caya di Solo 10, Noord* ☎ *297/586–7800 Ext. 229 / 230* ⊕ *www.tierradelsol.com.*

★ Fodor'sChoice **Pure Indulgence Spa.** Enjoy a new spa menu at Divi Phoenix's signature spa, which offers luxurious treat-ments with names that make them sound good enough to eat and drink. How about a Merlot massage or a wrap with fragrant notes of butternut cream cake? Couples can enjoy the private Lover's Suite with Jacuzzi baths, a steam room, and premium Hansgrohe rain showers. ⊠ *Divi Phoe-nix Aruba Beach Resort, J.E. Irausquin 75, Palm Beach* ☎ *297/586–6606* ⊕ *www.purespaaruba.com.*

The Ritz-Carlton Spa. Natural elements are the main theme at this upscale new spa with signature treatments revolv-ing around earth, sky, fire, and water. Local and natural ingredients have been incorporated wherever possible, such as Aruban honey in the *Candela Deseo* scrub, the *Dushi Terra* treatment that uses local black stones for massage, and the Awa awakening water treatment that infuses oils from local flowers for massage. There are

9

also soothing hydrotherapy options on-site. The spa has 13 treatment rooms and an adjoining fitness center with daily classes, including yoga and personal trainers. ✉ *Ritz-Carlton Aruba, L. G. Smith Blvd. 107, Palm Beach* ☎ *297/527–2222* ⊕ *www.ritzcarlton.com.*

ZoiA Spa. It's all about indulgence at the Hyatt's upscale spa, named after the Papiamento word for balance. Gentle music and the scent of botanicals make the world back home fade into the background. Newly arrived visitors to the island can opt for the jet lag massage that combines reflexology and aromatherapy, and those with the budget and time for a full day of relaxation can opt for the Serene package. There's even a mother-to-be package available. Island brides can avail themselves of a full menu of beauty services ranging from botanical facials (using local ingredients) to a full makeup job for the big day. The Pure High Tea package offers a delicious assortment of snacks and teas along with an hour of treatments. ✉ *Hyatt Regency Aruba Beach Resort & Casino, J.E. Irausquin Blvd. 85, Palm Beach* ☎ *297/586–1234* ⊕ *www.aruba.hyatt.com.*

TRAVEL SMART
ARUBA

GETTING HERE AND AROUND

Aruba is a small island, so it's virtually impossible to get lost when exploring. Most activities take place in and around Oranjestad or in the two main hotel areas, which are designated as the "low-rise" and "high-rise" areas. Main roads on the island are generally excellent, but getting to some of the more secluded beaches or historic sites will involve driving on unpaved tracks. Though Aruba is an arid island, there are occasional periods of heavy rain, and it's best to avoid exploring the national park or other wilderness areas during these times, since roads can become flooded, and muddy conditions can make driving treacherous.

▮ AIR TRAVEL

Aruba is 2½ hours from Miami; 4½ hours from New York; 5 hours from Boston, Chicago, Atlanta, or Toronto. Shorter still is the ¼- to ½-hour hop (depending on whether you take a prop or a jet plane) from Curaçao to Aruba.

Contacts Transportation Security Administration. ⊕ www.tsa.gov.

AIRPORTS

The island's Queen Beatrix International Airport (AUA) has been recently revamped and is equipped with thorough security, lots of flight displays, and state-of-the-art baggage-handling systems, shopping, and food-and-drink emporiums. There's also airportwide free Wi-Fi and new VIP club lounges.

Contacts Aeropuerto Internacional Reina Beatrix. ⊠ Wayaca z/n ☎ 297/524–2424 ⊕ www.airportaruba.com.

GROUND TRANSPORTATION

A taxi from the airport to most hotels takes about 20 minutes. It'll cost $22 to $25 to get to the hotels along Eagle Beach, $25 to $28 to the high-rise hotels on Palm Beach, and $18 to the hotels downtown (rates are a few dollars higher at night). You'll find a taxi stand right outside the baggage-claim area. Aruba taxis are not metered; they operate on a flat rate by destination. See ⊕ www.aruba.com/things-to-do/taxis-and-limousine-services for more information on rates.

For a pdf of rates see ⊕ www.aruba.com/sigma/Aruba_Taxi_Fares.pdf.

FLIGHTS

Many airlines fly nonstop to Aruba from several cities in North America; connections will usually be at a U.S. airport.

There are nonstop flights from Atlanta (Delta), Baltimore (Southwest), Boston (American, JetBlue, US Airways), Charlotte (American), Chicago (United), Fort Lauderdale (Spirit, JetBlue), Houston (Southwest, United), Miami (American, Aruba Airlines), Newark (United), Minneapolis (Delta), New York–JFK (American, Delta, JetBlue), New York–Newark (United),

Orlando (Southwest), Philadelphia (American), and Washington, D.C.–Dulles (United). Seasonal nonstops from major Canadian cities are available from WestJet and Air Canada and charter airlines like Sunwing and Air Transat.

Because of pre-U.S. customs clearance, you really need three hours before departure from Aruba's airport. Beyond typical check-in lines—unless you check in online and do not have baggage—you must go through two separate security checks and customs as well, and sometimes even random baggage checks. The entire procedure takes a lot of time, and there are not often enough customs agents on duty to handle all the traffic, especially on weekends. So be there early. The good news is that you do not have to deal with customs in the United States on the other end. The airport departure tax is included in the price of your ticket.

Contacts **Air Canada.**
☎ 888/247–2262 in North America ⊕ www.aircanada.com. **Air Transat.** ☎ 877/872–6728 ⊕ www.airtransat.com. **American Airlines.** ☎ 297/582–2700 on Aruba, 800/433–7300 ⊕ www.aa.com. **Delta Airlines.** ☎ 800/221–1212 ⊕ www.delta.com. **JetBlue.** ☎ 800/449–2525 ⊕ www.jetblue.com. **Southwest Airlines.** ☎ 800/435–9792 ⊕ www.southwest.com. **Spirit Airlines.** ☎ 801/401–2222 ⊕ www.spiritair.com. **Sunwing Airlines.** ☎ 800/877–1755 ⊕ www.sunwing.ca. **United Airlines.** ☎ 800/864–8331 ⊕ www.united.com. **Westjet.** ☎ 888/937–8538 ⊕ www.westjet.com/en-ca.

▌ BUS TRAVEL

Arubus N.V. is Aruba's public transportation company. Island buses are clean, well-maintained, sometimes air-conditioned, and regularly scheduled; they provide a safe, economical way to travel along the resort beaches all the way to the downtown Oranjestad main terminal. They stop at almost all major resorts and are a great way to hop into town for groceries to bring back to your hotel without taking expensive taxis. They run until fairly late at night and later on weekends. If you plan to take multiple trips in one day, purchase a day pass for US$10 at the main terminal in downtown Oranjestad for unlimited access to all their routes. Drivers give change if you don't have the exact fare (no large bills, though) and accept U.S. currency (but give change in florins). A one-way fare is US$2.60, and you can buy a return (round-trip) to Oranjestad for $5. Return bus fares to San Nicolas and Baby Beach from downtown are $8. Get all the updated information on rates, schedules, and routes on their website because things change often.

Contacts **Arubus.** ⊕ www.arubus.com.

▌ CAR TRAVEL

Driving is on the right, just as in the U.S. Most of Aruba's major attractions are fairly easy to find, and there are great maps all over the island to find out-of-the-way spots (mapping apps can also help). International traffic signs and Dutch-style traffic signals (with an extra light for a turning lane) can be confusing, though, if you're not used to them; use extreme caution, especially at intersections, until you grasp the rules of the road.

GASOLINE

Gas prices average a little more than $1.06 a liter (roughly a quarter of a gallon), which is reasonable by Caribbean standards but more expensive than in the U.S. Stations are plentiful in and near Oranjestad, San Nicolas, and Santa Cruz, and near the major high-rise hotels on the west coast. All take cash, and most take major credit cards. Nevertheless, gas prices aren't posted prominently, since they're fixed and the same at all stations.

PARKING

There are parking meters in downtown Oranjestad, but finding an open spot is very difficult, especially now that a lot of downtown is closed to vehicular traffic because of the eco-trolley and new pedestrian malls, but there is free parking behind the Renaissance Marketplace, where you may find a space if you are lucky. Otherwise, most parking is metered, and meters take U.S. coins, or you can pay with a smartcard (purchased at the Aruparking office in Oranjestad) or with the AruPark app.

Contacts Aruparking. ✉ *Wilhelminastraat 13, Oranjestad* ⊕ *www. aruparking.com.*

RENTAL CARS

In Aruba you must meet the minimum age requirements of each rental service. (Budget, for example, requires drivers to be over 25; Avis, over 23; some local operators over 25). A credit card (with a sufficient line of credit available) or a cash deposit of $500 is required. Rates vary seasonally and are usually lower from local agencies, but shopping for bargains and reserving a car online is a good strategy regardless of which company you rent from. Insurance is available starting at about $10 per day. Most visitors pick up their rental car at the airport, where you'll find both local and international brands; most companies have offices right across the road from the airport exit (⊕ *www.airportaruba.com/ car-rental*), but there are branches all over the island, including at major resorts. Most companies offer free drop-off and pickup at your hotel if you aren't renting a car on arrival. You can ask the concierge of your hotel or the front desk to recommend a local rental if you only want one for a day to tour the island. Opt for a four-wheel drive vehicle if you plan to explore the outback and go off the beaten path.

Contacts Avis. ☎ *297/582–5496 in Aruba, 800/532–1527* ⊕ *www. avis.com.* **Amigo.** ☎ *297/583–8833* ⊕ *www.amigocar.com.* **Budget.** ☎ *297/582–8600, 800/472–3325 in Aruba* ⊕ *www.budgetaruba.com.* **Thrifty.** ☎ *297/583–4902* ⊕ *www. thriftycarrentalaruba.com.* **Tropic**

Car Rental. ☎ *297/583–7336*
⊕ *www.tropiccurrent-aruba.com.*

RENTAL-CAR INSURANCE

Everyone who rents a car wonders whether the insurance that the rental companies offer is worth the expense. No one—including us—has a simple answer. If you own a car, your personal auto insurance may cover a rental to some degree, though not all policies protect you abroad; always read your policy's fine print. If you don't have auto insurance, then seriously consider buying the collision- or loss-damage waiver (CDW or LDW) from the car-rental company, which eliminates your liability for damage to the car. Some credit cards offer CDW coverage, but it's usually supplemental to your own insurance and rarely covers SUVs, mini-vans, or luxury models. If your coverage is secondary, you may still be liable for loss-of-use costs from the car-rental company. But no credit-card insurance is valid unless you use that card for *all* transactions, from reserving to paying the final bill. It's sometimes cheaper to buy insurance as part of your general travel-insurance policy.

ROADSIDE EMERGENCIES

Discuss with the rental-car agency what to do in the case of an emergency. Make sure you understand what your insurance covers and what it doesn't; let someone at your accommodations know where you're heading and when you plan to return. If you find yourself stranded, hail a taxi or speak to the locals, who may have some helpful advice about finding your way to a phone or a bus stop. Keep emergency numbers with you, just in case. Because Aruba is such a small island, you should never panic if you have car trouble; it's likely you'll be within relatively easy walking distance of a populated area.

ROAD CONDITIONS

Aside from the major highways, some of the island's winding roads are poorly marked (although the situation is slowly improving). Keep an eye out for rocks and other debris when driving on remote roads. When in the countryside, also keep your eyes open for wild goats and donkeys that might wander onto the road.

RULES OF THE ROAD

Driving here is on the right side of the road, American-style. Despite the laid-back ways of locals, when they get behind the steering wheel they often speed and take liberties with road rules, especially outside the more heavily traveled Oranjestad and hotel areas. Keep a watchful eye for passing cars and for vehicles coming out of side roads. Speed limits are rarely posted, but the maximum speed is 60 kph (40 mph) and 40 kph (25 mph) through settlements. Speed limits and the use of seat belts are enforced.

▮ TAXI TRAVEL

You'll find taxis at the airport and also at all major resorts (ask if you need one to be called). You don't really hail cabs in Aruba; if you need one, just go to the nearest hotel, and the doorman will get you one. Your restaurant or bar will also call one for you. In downtown Oranjestad, taxis are always to be found around the Renaissance Marina lower lobby. Taxi rates in Aruba are fixed (i.e., there are no meters; the rates are set by the government and displayed on a chart by zone) and are posted on the Aruba Tourism Authority website, though you should confirm the fare with your driver before your ride begins. Add $2 to the fare after midnight and $2 to $4 on Sunday and holidays.

Contacts Arubas Transfer Tour & Taxi C.A. ✉ *Airport* ☎ *297/582-2116, 297/582-2010* ⊕ *www.airportaruba.com/taxi-transportation.*

ESSENTIALS

ACCOMMODATIONS

Most Aruba hotels are found in two clusters: the low-rise hotels in a stretch along Druif Beach and Eagle Beach, and the high-rise hotels on a stretch of Palm Beach. With a few exceptions, the hotels in the high-rise area tend to be larger and more expensive than their low-rise counterparts, but they usually offer a wider range of services.

When making your reservations, be sure you understand how much you are really paying before finalizing any reservation. Hotels collect 9.5% in taxes (2% of which goes to marketing to tourists) on top of a typical 11% service charge, for a total of 20.5%. An additional $3 Environmental Levy per day was added in 2013.

Some resorts will allow you to cancel without any kind of penalty—even if you prepaid to secure a discounted rate—if you cancel at least 24 hours in advance. Others require you to cancel a week in advance or penalize you the cost of one night. Small inns and bed-and-breakfasts are most likely to require you to cancel far in advance. Most hotels allow children under a certain age to stay in their parents' room at no extra charge, but others charge for them as extra adults; find out the cut-off age for discounts.

Not sure where to stay? The Aruba Tourism Authority has a comprehensive list of accommodations (⊕ *www.aruba.com*), and their staff members are always ready to help find accommodations to suit any budget.

■ TIP→ **Hotels have private bathrooms, phones, and TVs, and don't offer meals unless we specify a meal plan in the review (i.e., breakfast, some meals, all meals, all-inclusive). We always list facilities but not whether you'll be charged an extra fee to use them.**

For lodging price categories, consult the price chart at the beginning of the Where to Stay chapter.

APARTMENT AND HOUSE RENTALS

Apartments and time-share condos are common in Aruba. So if you're looking for more space for your family or group to spread out in (and especially if you want to have access to a kitchen to make some meals), this can be a very budget-friendly option. The money you save can be used for more dining and activities. Many time-share resorts are full-service, offering the same range of water sports and other activities as any other resort, and almost all of them offer unused units on their websites (some through third-party booking sites). And some regular resorts also have a time-share component. AirBnB (⊕ *www.airbnb.com*) also offers a wide range of rental options on the island.

▮ ADDRESSES

"Informal" might best describe Aruban addresses. Sometimes the street designation is in English (as in J. E. Irausquin Boulevard), other times in Dutch (as in Wilhelminastraat); sometimes it's not specified whether something is a boulevard or a *straat* (street) at all. Street numbers follow street names, and postal codes aren't used. In rural areas you might have to ask a local for directions—and be prepared for such instructions as "Take a right at the market, then a left where you see the big divi-divi tree."

▮ COMMUNICATIONS

INTERNET

Resortwide free Wi-Fi is common in Aruba. Nevertheless, some larger Aruba resort hotels offer it only in lobbies and on a few desktop computers in a business center and then charge daily rates for access in your room and other parts of the property. Many bars and dining spots and even stores now offer free Wi-Fi; just ask them for their password when you order or buy something. There are also free government-sponsored Wi-Fi hot spots and zones for tourists and locals with more to come.

PHONES

To call Aruba direct from the United States, dial 011–297, followed by the seven-digit number in Aruba.

LOCAL CALLS

Dial the seven-digit number.

CALLING THE UNITED STATES

Dial 0, then 1, the area code, and the number. AT&T customers can dial 800–8000 from special phones at the cruise dock and in the airport's arrival and departure halls and charge calls to their credit card.

MOBILE PHONES

Both SETAR and Digicel offer rental phones, but if you are staying for more than a week, it may be just as cost-effective to buy a cheap phone; even easier is buying a pre-paid local SIM and using it in your own unlocked phone. Most U.S.–based GSM and CDMA cell phones work on Aruba.

If you have a multiband phone (some countries use frequencies different from those used in the United States) and your service provider uses the world-standard GSM network (as do T-Mobile, AT&T, and Verizon), you can probably use your phone abroad. Roaming fees can be steep. And overseas you normally pay the toll charges for incoming calls. It's almost always cheaper to send a text message than to make a call.

▮TIP→ If you travel internationally frequently, save one of your old mobile phones or buy a cheap one on the Internet; ask your cell-phone company to unlock it for you, and take it with you as a travel phone, buying a new SIM card with pay-as-you-go service in each destination.

Contacts **Digicel.** ☎ 297/522–2222 ⊕ www.digicelaruba.com. **SETAR.** ☎ 297/525–1000 ⊕ www.setar.aw.

▮ CUSTOMS AND DUTIES

You can bring up to 1 liter of spirits, 3 liters of beer, or 2.25 liters of wine per person, and up to 200 cigarettes or 50 cigars into Aruba. You don't need to declare the value of gifts or other items, although customs officials may inquire about large items or large quantities of goods and charge (at their discretion) an import tax of 7.5% to 22% on items worth more than $230. Meat, birds, and illegal substances are forbidden. You may be asked to provide written verification that plants are free of diseases. If you're traveling with pets, bring a veterinarian's note attesting to their good health.

Contacts Aruba Customs Office. ☎ 297/582–1800 ⊕ *www.douane. aw/.*

▮ EATING OUT

Aruba offers a startling variety of eating options thanks to the tourist trade, with choices ranging from upscale to simple roadside dining. The island is also a particularly family-friendly destination, so bringing the kids along is rarely a problem, and many restaurants offer children's menus.

Unless otherwise noted, the restaurants listed in this guide are open daily for lunch and dinner.

ARUBAN CUISINE

Aruba shares many of its traditional foods with Bonaire and Curaçao. These dishes are a fusion of the various influences that have shaped the culture of the islands. Proximity to mainland South America means that many traditional snack and breakfast foods of Venezuelan origin, such as *empanadas* (fried cornmeal dumplings filled with ground meat), are widely found. The Dutch influence is evident in the fondness for cheese of all sorts, but especially Gouda. *Keshi yena,* ground meat or seafood with seasonings and placed in a hollowed-out cheese rind before baking, is a national dish.

If there's one thread that unites the cuisines of the Caribbean, it's cornmeal, and Arubans love nothing more than a side of *funchi* (like a thick polenta) or a *pan bati* (a fried cornmeal pancake) to make a traditional meal complete. Though Aruban cuisine isn't by nature spicy, it's almost always accompanied by a small bowl of spicy *pika* (a condiment of fiery hot peppers and onions in vinegar) or a bottle of hot sauce made from local peppers. An abundance of seafood means that seafood is the most popular protein on the island, and it's been said that if there were an Aruban national dish, it would be the catch of the day.

PAYING

We assume that restaurants and hotels accept credit cards. If they don't, we'll note it in the review.

RESERVATIONS AND DRESS

We mention reservations only when they're essential (there's no other way you'll ever get a table) or when they're not accepted. We mention dress only when men are required to wear a jacket or a jacket and tie.

WINES, BEER, AND SPIRITS

Arubans have a great love for wine, so even small supermarkets have a fairly good selection of European and South American wines at prices that are reasonable by Caribbean standards. The beer of choice in Aruba is the island-brewed Balashi and the newer Balashi Chill often served with a wedge of lime, and new local brands have also surfaced like Hopi Bon and Hopi Stout. Local spirits also include *ponce crema*, a wickedly potent eggnog type of liqueur.

▮ ELECTRICITY

Aruba runs on a 110-volt cycle, the same as in the United States; outlets are usually the two-prong variety. Total blackouts are rare, and most large hotels have backup generators.

▮ EMERGENCIES

The number to call in case of emergency—911—is the same as in the United States.

▮ HEALTH

As a rule, water is pure and food is wholesome in hotels and local restaurants throughout Aruba, but be cautious when buying food from street vendors. And just as you would at home, wash or peel all fruits and vegetables before eating them. Traveler's diarrhea, caused by consuming contaminated water, unpasteurized milk and milk products, and unrefrigerated food, isn't a big problem—unless it happens to you. So watch what you eat, especially at outdoor buffets in the

WORD OF MOUTH

Was the service stellar or not up to snuff? Did the food give you shivers of delight or leave you cold? Did the prices and portions make you happy or sad? Rate restaurants and write your own reviews in Travel Ratings or start a discussion about your favorite places in Travel Talk on www.fodors.com. Your comments might even appear in our books. Yes, you, too, can be a correspondent!

hot sun. Make sure cooked food is hot and cold food has been properly refrigerated.

The major health risk is sunburn or sunstroke. A long-sleeve shirt, a hat, and long pants or a beach wrap are essential on a boat, for midday at the beach, and whenever you go out sightseeing. Use sunscreen with an SPF of at least 15—especially if you're fair—and apply it liberally on your nose, ears, and other sensitive and exposed areas. Make sure the sunscreen is waterproof if you're engaging in water sports. Always limit your sun time for the first few days, and drink plenty of liquids. Limit intake of caffeine and alcohol, which hastens dehydration.

Mosquitoes can be bothersome, so pack strong repellent (the ones that contain DEET or Picaridin are the most effective). The strong trade winds generally keep them at bay during the day unless you are in thick foliage or mangrove areas near the water. It's at dusk when they come out, when winds calm, and at night when you are dining with toes in the sand. Zika and dengue have been reported on Aruba, but the island is not considered a high-risk zone. Protect yourself regardless.

Don't fly within 24 hours of scuba diving. In an emergency, Air Ambulance service will fly you to Curaçao at a low altitude if you need to get to a decompression chamber.

OVER-THE-COUNTER REMEDIES

There are a number of pharmacies and stores selling simple medications throughout the island (including at most hotels), and virtually anything obtainable in North America is available in Aruba.

SHOTS AND MEDICATIONS

No special vaccinations are required to visit Aruba.

Contacts Centers for Disease Control & Prevention (*CDC*). ☎ 877/394-8747 *international travelers' health line* ⊕ www.cdc.gov/travel. **World Health Organization** (*WHO*). ⊕ www.who.int.

▮ HOURS OF OPERATION

Most of Aruba's services like banks are basically open the same times as you'd expect in North America, though some spots will close on Sunday and on national holidays. Most modern conveniences are available seven days a week.

HOLIDAYS

Aruba's official holidays are New Year's Day, Good Friday, Easter Sunday, and Christmas, as well as Betico Croes Day (January 25), National Anthem and Flag Day (March 18), King's Day (April 30), Labor Day (May 1), and Ascension Day (39 days after Easter).

▮ MAIL

From Aruba to the United States or Canada a letter costs Afl2.20 (about $1.25) and a postcard costs Afl1.30 (75¢). Expect it to take one to two weeks. When addressing letters to Aruba, don't worry about the lack of formal addresses or postal codes; the island's postal service knows where to go.

If you need to send a package in a hurry, there are a few options. FedEx offers overnight service to the United States if you get your package in before 3 pm; there is a convenient office in downtown Oranjestad. Another big courier service is UPS, and several smaller local courier services, most of them open weekdays 9 to 5, also provide international deliveries. Check the local phone book for details.

Contacts FedEx. ✉ *FedEx World Service Center, Wayaca 31-A, Oranjestad* ☎ 297/592-9039 ⊕ www.fedex.com. **UPS.** ✉ *L. G. Smith Blvd. 128, Oranjestad* ☎ 297/588-0640 ⊕ www.ups.com.

▮ MONEY

Arubans happily accept U.S. dollars virtually everywhere, so most travelers will find no real need to exchange money, except for necessary pocket change (for soda machines or pay phones). The official currency is the Aruban florin (Afl), also called the guilder, which is made up of 100 cents. Silver coins come in denominations of 1, 2½, 5, 10, 25, and 50 (the square one) cents. Paper currency comes in denominations of 5, 10, 25, 50, and 100 florins.

Prices quoted throughout this book are in U.S. dollars unless otherwise noted.

Prices throughout this guide are given for adults. Substantially reduced fees are almost always available for children, students, and seniors.

ATMS AND BANKS

If you need fast cash, you'll find ATMs that accept international cards (and dispense cash in both U.S. and local currency) at banks in Oranjestad, at the major malls, and along the roads leading to the hotel strip.

Contacts **Caribbean Mercantile Bank.** ⌧ *Palm Beach 4B, Noord* ☎ *297/582–4373* ⊕ *www.cmbnv.com.* **Aruba RBC Bank.** ⌧ *Caya G. F. Betico Croes 89, Oranjestad* ☎ *297/588–0101* ⊕ *aw.rbcnetbank.com.*

CREDIT CARDS

It's a good idea to inform your credit-card company before you travel, especially if you're going abroad and don't travel internationally very often. Otherwise, the credit-card company might put a hold on your card owing to unusual activity—not a good thing halfway through your trip. Record all your credit-card numbers—as well as the phone numbers to call if your cards are lost or stolen—in a safe place, so you're prepared should something go wrong. Both MasterCard and Visa have general numbers you can call (collect if you're abroad) if your card is lost, but you're better off calling the number of your issuing bank, since MasterCard and Visa usually just transfer you to your bank; your bank's number is usually printed on your card.

Although it's usually cheaper (and safer) to use a credit card abroad for large purchases (so you can cancel payments or be reimbursed if there's a problem), note that some credit-card companies *and* the banks that issue them add substantial percentages to all foreign transactions, whether they're in a foreign currency or not. Check on these fees before leaving home, so there won't be any surprises when you get the bill.

Contacts **American Express.** ☎ *800/528–4800 in U.S., 336/393–1111 collect from abroad* ⊕ *www.americanexpress.com.* **MasterCard.** ☎ *800/627–8372 in U.S., 636/722–7111 collect from abroad* ⊕ *www.mastercard.com.* **Visa.** ☎ *800/847–2911 in U.S., 800–1518 aruba* ⊕ *www.visa.com.*

▮ PACKING

Dress on Aruba is generally casual. Bring loose-fitting clothing made of natural fabrics to see you through days of heat and humidity. Pack a beach cover-up, both to protect yourself from the sun and to provide something to wear to and from your hotel room. Bathing suits and immodest attire are frowned upon away from the beach. A sun hat is advisable, but you don't have to pack one—inexpensive straw hats are available everywhere. For shopping and sightseeing, bring shorts, jeans, T-shirts, long-sleeve cotton shirts, slacks, and sundresses. Nighttime dress can range from very informal to casually elegant, depending on the establishment. A tie is practically never required, but a jacket may be appropriate in fancy restaurants. You may need a light sweater or jacket for evening.

PASSPORTS AND VISAS

A valid passport is required to enter or reenter the United States from Aruba.

RESTROOMS

Outside Oranjestad, the public restrooms can be found in dining and small restaurants that dot the countryside.

SAFETY

Arubans are very friendly, so you needn't be afraid to stop and ask anyone for directions. It's a relatively safe island, but commonsense rules still apply. Lock your rental car when you leave it, and leave valuables in your hotel safe. Don't leave bags unattended in the airport, on the beach, or on tour vehicles.

■ TIP→ **Distribute your cash, credit cards, IDs, and other valuables between a deep front pocket, an inside jacket or vest pocket, and a hidden money pouch.**

TAXES

For purchases you'll pay a 1.5% BBO tax (a turnover tax on each level of sale for all goods and services) in all but the duty-free shops.

TIME

Aruba is in the Atlantic standard time zone, which is one hour later than eastern standard time or four hours earlier than Greenwich mean time. During daylight saving time, between March and October, Atlantic standard is the same time as eastern daylight time.

Time Zones **Timeanddate.com.**
⊕ *www.timeanddate.com/worldclock.*

TIPPING

Restaurants sometimes include a 10%–15% service charge on the bill; when in doubt, ask. If service isn't included, a tip of at least 15% is standard; if it's included, it's still customary to add something extra, usually small change, at your discretion. Taxi drivers expect a 10%–15% tip, but it isn't mandatory. Porters and bellhops should receive about $2 per bag; chambermaids about $4 a day, but check to see if their tips are included in your bill so you don't overpay.

TRIP INSURANCE

Comprehensive travel policies typically cover trip cancellation and interruption, letting you cancel or cut your trip short because of a personal emergency, illness, or, in some cases, acts of terrorism in your destination. Such policies also cover evacuation and medical care.

Some also cover you for trip delays because of bad weather or mechanical problems as well as for lost or delayed baggage. Another type of coverage to look for is financial default—that is, when your trip is disrupted because a tour operator, airline, or cruise line goes out of business. Generally you must buy this when you book your trip or shortly thereafter, and it's available to you only if your operator isn't on a list of excluded companies.

At the very least, consider buying medical-only coverage. Neither Medicare nor some private insurers cover medical expenses anywhere outside the United States (including time aboard a cruise ship, even if it leaves from a U.S. port). Medical-only policies typically reimburse you for medical care (excluding that related to pre-existing conditions) and hospitalization abroad, and provide for evacuation. You still have to pay the bills and await reimbursement from the insurer, though.

Another option is to sign up with a medical-evacuation assistance company. A membership in one of these companies gets you doctor referrals, emergency evacuation or repatriation, 24-hour hotlines for medical consultation, and other assistance. International SOS Assistance Emergency and AirMed International provide evacuation services and medical referrals. MedjetAssist offers medical evacuation.

Expect comprehensive travel insurance policies to cost about 4% to 8% of the total price of your trip (it's more like 8%–12% if you're over age 70). A medical-only policy may or may not be cheaper than a comprehensive policy. Always read the fine print of your policy to make sure that you're covered for the risks that are of most concern to you. Compare several policies to make sure you're getting the best price and range of coverage available.

Comprehensive Travel Insurers AIG Travel Guard. ☎ 800/826–4919 ⊕ www.travelguard.com. **CSA Travel Protection.** ☎ 800/348–9505 in U.S. ⊕ www.csatravelprotection.com. **HTH Worldwide.** ☎ 888/243–2358 ⊕ www.hthworldwide.com. **Travelex Insurance.** ☎ 888/228–9792 ⊕ www.travelex-insurance.com. **Travel Insured International.** ☎ 800/243–3174 ⊕ www.travelinsured.com.

Insurance Comparison Sites Insure My Trip.com. ☎ 800/551–1337 ⊕ www.insuremytrip.com. **Square Mouth.com.** ☎ 800/240–0369 ⊕ www.squaremouth.com.

Medical Assistance Companies AirMed International Medical Group. ☎ 800/356–2161 ⊕ www.airmed.com. **International SOS.** ☎ 215/942–8226 ⊕ www.internationalsos.com. **MedjetAssist.** ☎ 800/527–7478 ⊕ www.medjetassist.com.

Medical-Only Insurers International Medical Group. ☎ 800/628–4664 ⊕ www.imglobal.com. **Wallach & Company.** ☎ 800/237–6615 ⊕ www.wallach.com.

▌ VISITOR INFORMATION

Before leaving home, research online about all Aruba has to offer at their tourism authority's website aruba.com. They also have a handy app you can download to your smartphone.

Contacts **Aruba Tourism Authority.** ⊠ *L.G. Smith Blvd. 8, Oranjestad* ☎ *800/862–7822 in the U.S./international, 297/582–3777 in Aruba* ⊕ *www.aruba.com.*

▌ WEDDINGS

People over the age of 18 can marry as long as they submit the appropriate documents 14 days in advance. Couples are required to submit birth certificates with raised seals, through the mail or in person, to Aruba's Office of the Civil Registry. They also need an apostil—a document proving they're free to marry—from their country of residence. Same-sex ceremonies are also available on Aruba, though they're not legally binding.

With so many beautiful spots to choose from, weddings on Aruba are guaranteed to be romantic.

Aruba Weddings for You. The official wedding-planning service of the Divi family of resorts on Aruba, this is a full-service operation that can take care of everything from scouting the location to arranging a trash-the-dress photo shoot. Specializing in romantic beach weddings, they can also help with all the paperwork and the planning with a civil ceremony package. ☎ *297/525–5293* ⊕ *www.arubaweddingsforyou.com.*

Fodor'sChoice **Aruba Fairy Tales Weddings.** Founder Indira Maduro has been planning weddings on Aruba for more than a decade, helping visitors tie the knot or renew their vows on the island's most beautiful beaches in high style. Recently her company has branched out to also specialize in LGBT weddings under the name G+L Weddings, provided as a separate service. They can plan pre- and post-wedding activities on the island for your group as well. ☎ *297/993–0045, 297/593–0045* ⊕ *arubafairytales.com.*

INDEX

PHOTO CREDITS

Front cover: Jane Sweeney / AWL Images [Description: Caribbean, Netherland Antilles, Aruba, Flamingo beach]. 1, Holger W./Shutterstock. 2, Corey Weiner / Red Square, Inc. 3, (top), Göran Ingman / Flickr, [CC BY-542.0] 3 (bottom), Red Square, Inc. 4 (top), Aruba Tourism Authority. 4 (bottom), Courtesy of Kukoo Kunuku. 5 (top), Rebecca Genin/Aruba Tourism. 5 (bottom) and 6 (top), Aruba Tourism Authority. 6 (bottom), Passions on the Beach. 7, Vilainecrevette/Shutterstock. 8 (top), Jack Jackson / age fotostock. 8 (bottom), Aruba Tourism Authority. 10, Corey Weiner/redsquarephoto.com/Marriott. **Chapter 1: Experience Aruba:** 12-13, Aruba Tourism Authority. 22, David P. Smith/Shutterstock. **Chapter 2: Exploring:** 23, Aruba Tourism Authority. 28-29, Donaldford I Dreamstime.com. 38, Sarah Bossert/iStockphoto. 40-41, Kjorgen I Dreamstime.com. 42, Aruba Tourism Authority. 46-47, Paul D'Innocenzo. **Chapter 3: Beaches:** 49, Zazen I Dreamstime.com. 52-53, Marriott. 57, Kjersti Joergensen/Shutterstock. **Chapter 4: Where to Eat:** 59, Madame Janette's. 66, Kenneth Theysen I Timeless-Pixx. 72, Madame Janette's. **Chapter 5: Where to Stay:** 81, Corey Weiner/redsquarephoto. com/Marriott. 85, Marriott. 88, Bucuti Beach Resort. 90-91, Famke Backx/ iStockphoto. 92, Amsterdam Manor Beach Resort Aruba. 94, Corey Weiner/ redsquarephoto.com/Marriott. **Chapter 6: Nightlife and Performing Arts:** 97, Bas Rabeling/Shutterstock. 100-101, Stuart Pearce / age fotostock. 103, Aruba Tourism Authority. **Chapter 7: Casinos:** 111, Aruba Tourism Authority. 113, The Ritz Carlton, Aruba. 117, Corey Weiner/redsquarephoto.com/Marriott. 120, Aruba Marriott Stellaris Casino & Resort. **Chapter 8: Sports and the Outdoors:** 127, Aruba Tourism Authority. 129 and 132, Corey Weiner/redsquarephoto.com/ Marriott. 138, Marriott. 142-143, Svitlana Prada/iStockphoto. 144, Rebecca Genin/Aruba Tourism. 148, Paul D'Innocenzo. **Chapter 9: Shopping:** 151, mandritoiu / Shutterstock.com. 158, madmack66/Flickr. 164, Aruba Tourism Authority. Spine: Littleny I Dreamstime.com.

About Our Writer: Photo of Susan Campbell, courtesy of Aldrich Herelijn.

NOTES

NOTES

NOTES

NOTES

Fodor's InFocus ARUBA

Editorial: Douglas Stallings, *Editorial Director*; Margaret Kelly, Jacinta O'Halloran, *Senior Editors*; Kayla Becker, Alexis Kelly, Amanda Sadlowski, *Editors*; Teddy Minford, *Content Editor*; Rachael Roth, *Content Manager*

Design: Tina Malaney, *Design and Production Director*; Jessica Gonzalez, *Production Designer*

Photography: Jennifer Arnow, *Senior Photo Editor*

Maps: Rebecca Baer, *Senior Map Editor*; David Lindroth, Ed Jacobus, with additional cartography provided by Henry Columb, Mark Stroud, and Ali Baird, Moon Street Cartography, *Cartographers*

Production: Jennifer DePrima, *Editorial Production Manager*; Carrie Parker, *Senior Production Editor*; Elyse Rozelle, *Production Editor*

Business & Operations: Chuck Hoover, *Chief Marketing Officer*; Joy Lai, *Vice President and General Manager*; Stephen Horowitz, *Director of Business Development and Revenue Operations*; Tara McCrillis, *Director of Publishing Operations*; Eliza D. Aceves, *Content Operations Manager and Strategist*

Public Relations and Marketing: Joe Ewaskiw, *Manager*; Esther Su, *Marketing Manager*

Writer: Susan Campbell

Editor: Douglas Stallings

Production Editor: Carrie Parker

6th Edition

ISBN 978-1-64097-050-2

ISSN 1939–988X

All details in this book are based on information supplied to us at press time. Always confirm information when it matters, especially if you're making a detour to visit a specific place. Fodor's expressly disclaims any liability, loss, or risk, personal or otherwise, that is incurred as a consequence of the use of any of the contents of this book.

SPECIAL SALES

This book is available at special discounts for bulk purchases for sales promotions or premiums. For more information, e-mail SpecialMarkets@fodors.com.

PRINTED IN THE UNITED STATES OF AMERICA

10 9 8 7 6 5 4 3 2 1

ABOUT OUR WRITER

Based in Montreal, Canada, Susan Campbell is an award-winning travel writer. She has been an expert on the Dutch Caribbean for over 20 years and is the major contributor to the on-island guides of Aruba, Bonaire, Curacao and St. Maarten for Nights Publications. Susan visits Aruba several times a year and has extensive knowledge of the island and its culture, history, and attractions, which she shares via multiple online and print outlets throughout North America.

EUGENE FODOR

Hungarian-born Eugene Fodor (1905–91) began his travel career as an interpreter on a French cruise ship. The experience inspired him to write *On the Continent* (1936), the first guidebook to receive annual updates and discuss a country's way of life as well as its sights. Fodor later joined the U.S. Army and worked for the OSS in World War II. After the war, he kept up his intelligence work while expanding his guidebook series. During the Cold War, many guides were written by fellow agents who understood the value of insider information. Today's guides continue Fodor's legacy by providing travelers with timely coverage, insider tips, and cultural context.